COLORFUL MEMORIES

A coloring book of poetry and illustrations inspired
by the Day of the Dead tradition

||||||||||||||||||
I0480885

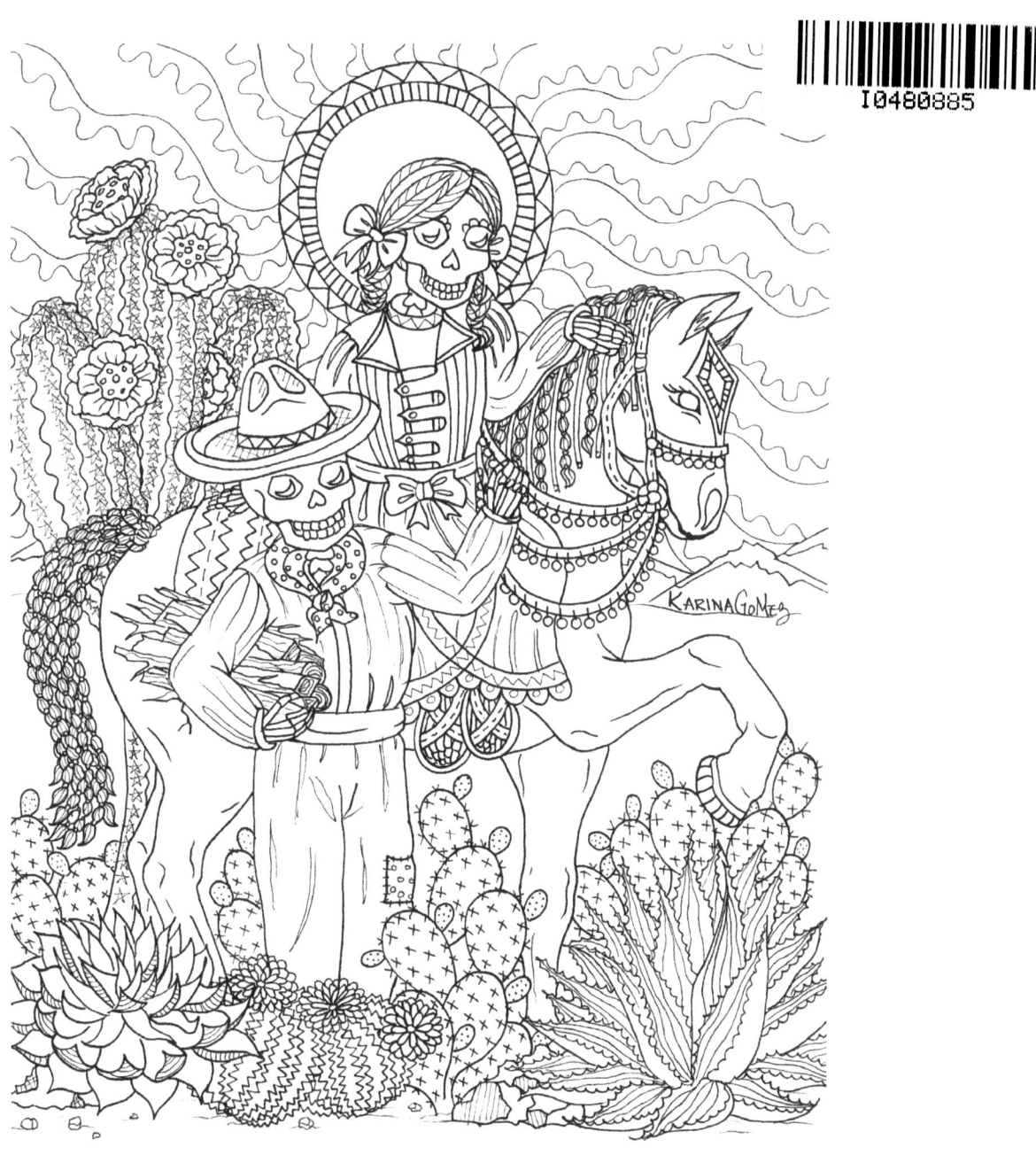

Illustrations by Karina Gómez and Laura Gómez
Poetry by Amelia Orozco

We dedicate this book to our families and friends
who have stood by us through the years,
and who form part of our stories.

Index

I
The Rhythm of my Senses

Tamales, sugar cane and pastries, too
They call us and invite us,
They are like a dinner bell tune!

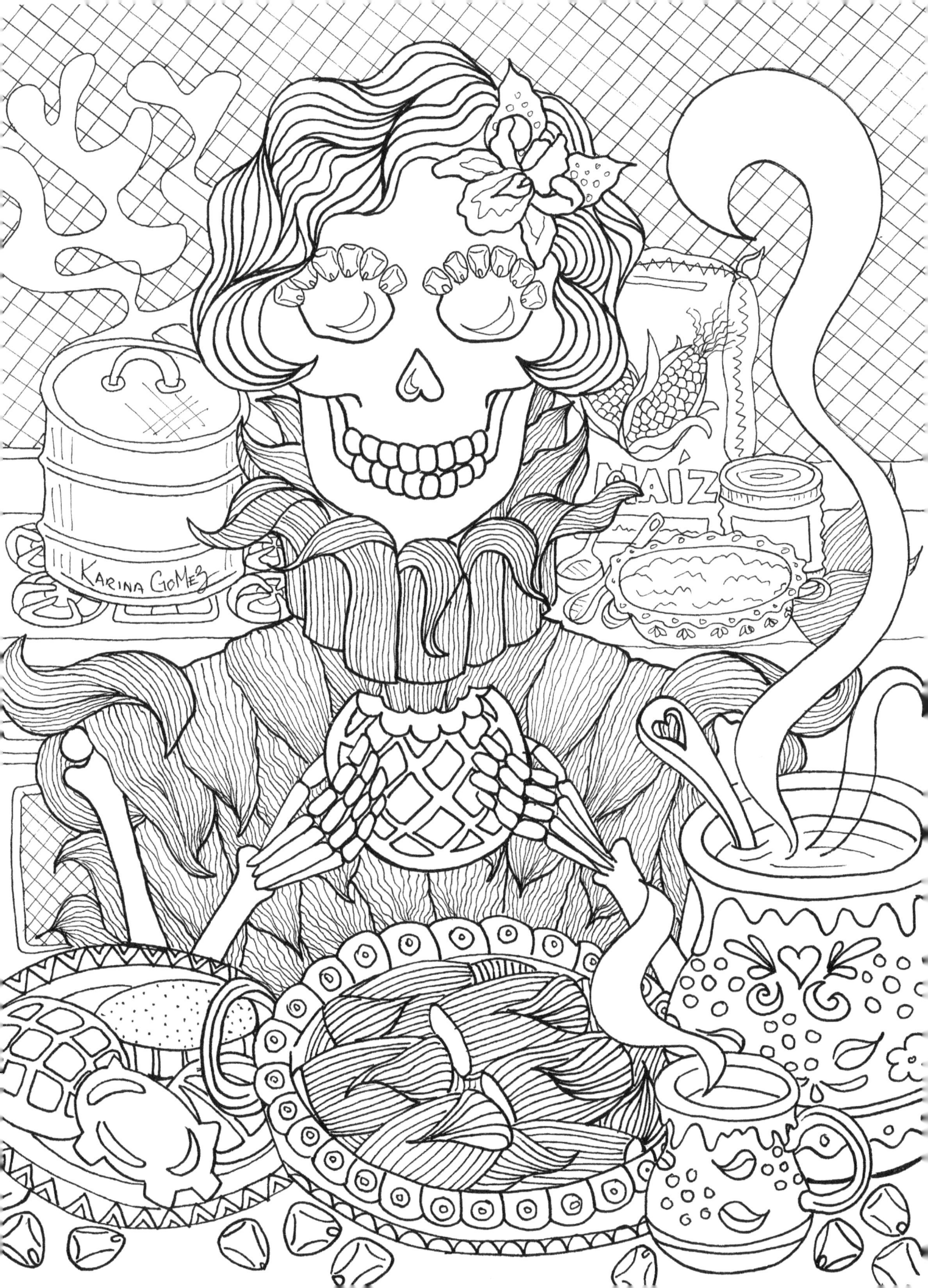

Cinnamon is like a guitar strumming with love
Red chili peppers dance to the beat of a drum
Maize rattles and shakes not missing a beat

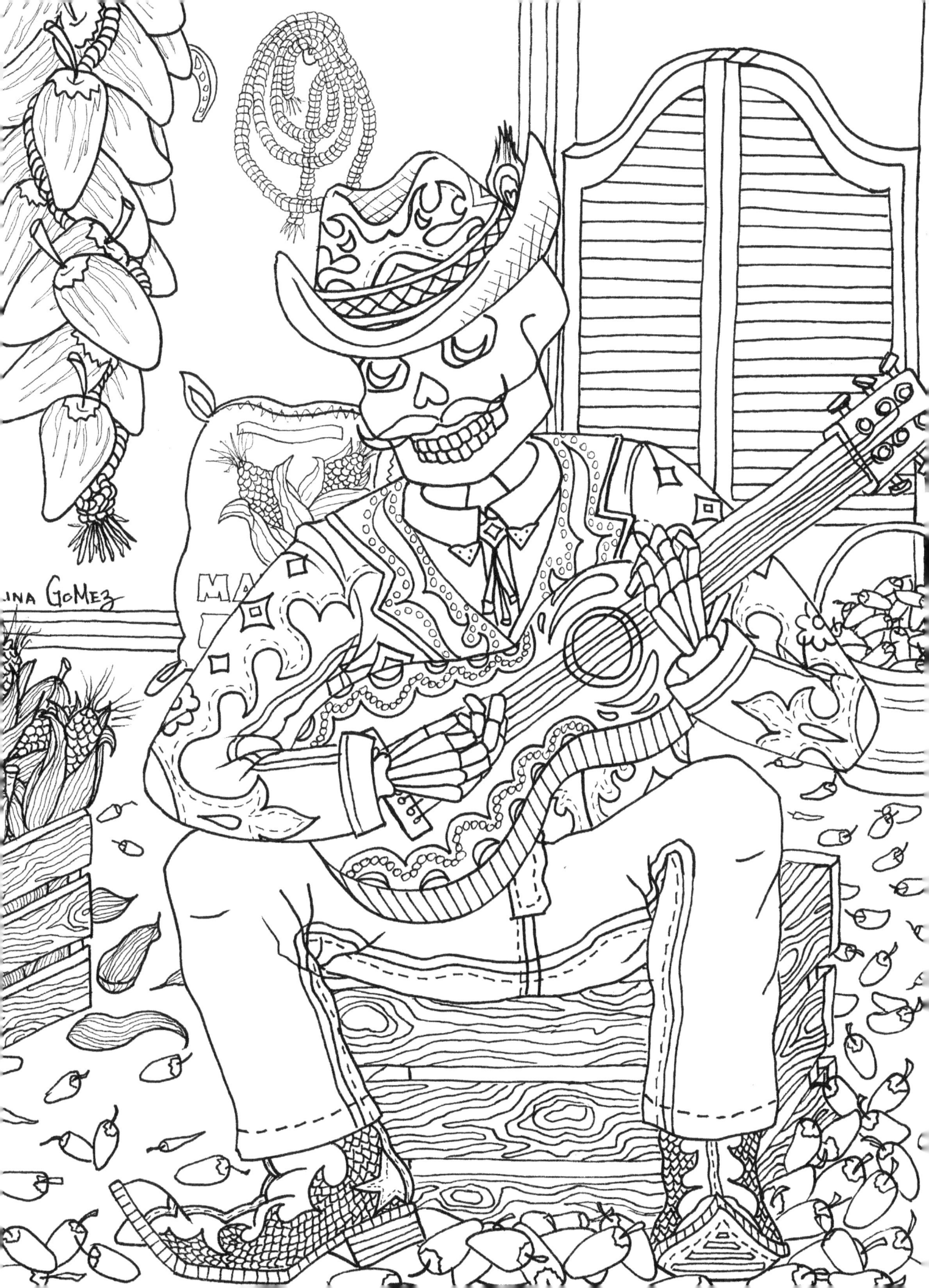

The family spins the plates around
The spoons sing along
Even the cups laugh and dance
Everyone joyfully sings
Young and old, all join in.

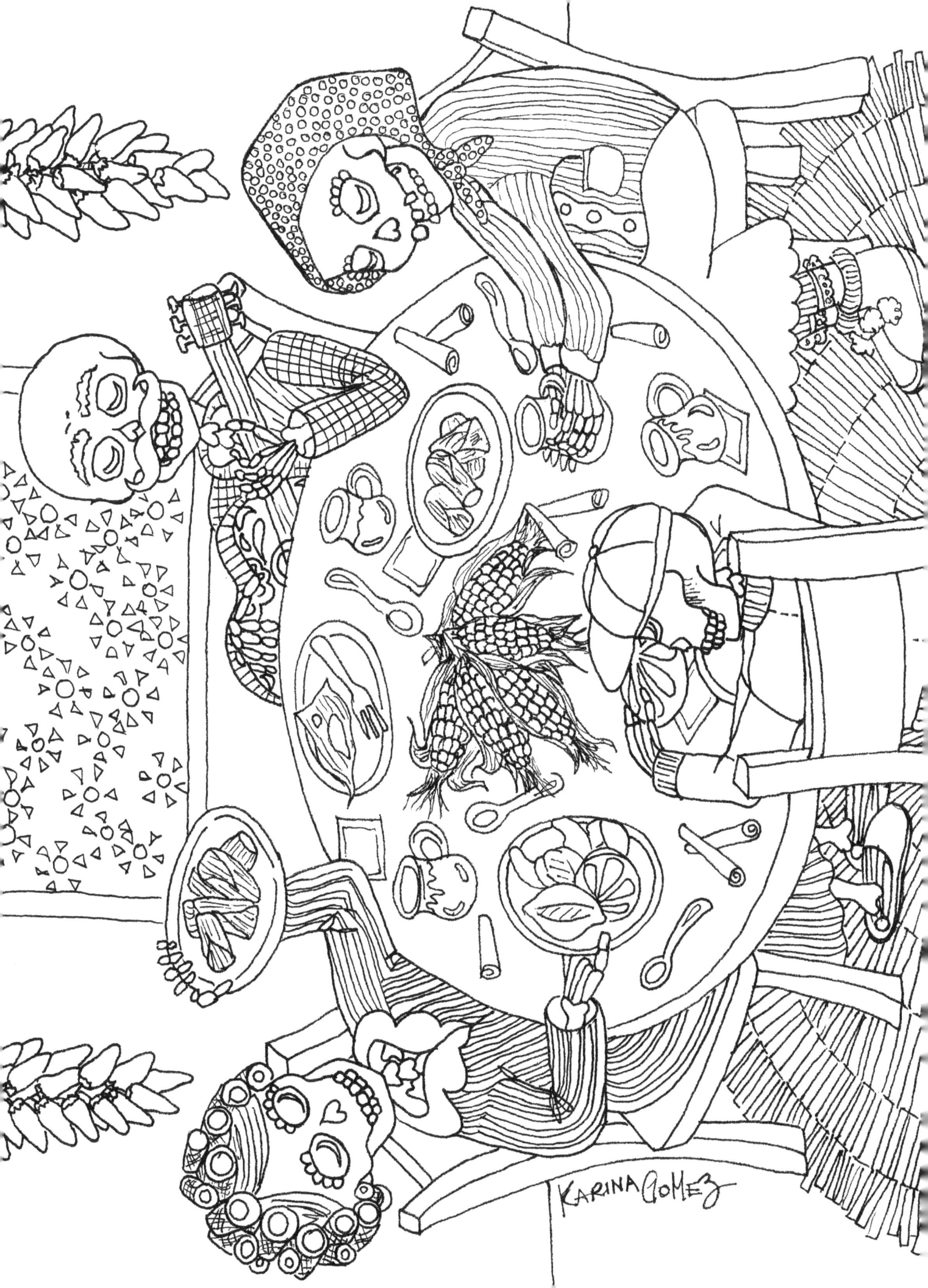

Like a tired old record
The music starts to fade
Everyone anticipates warm frothy milk
Kissed with a dollop of coffee

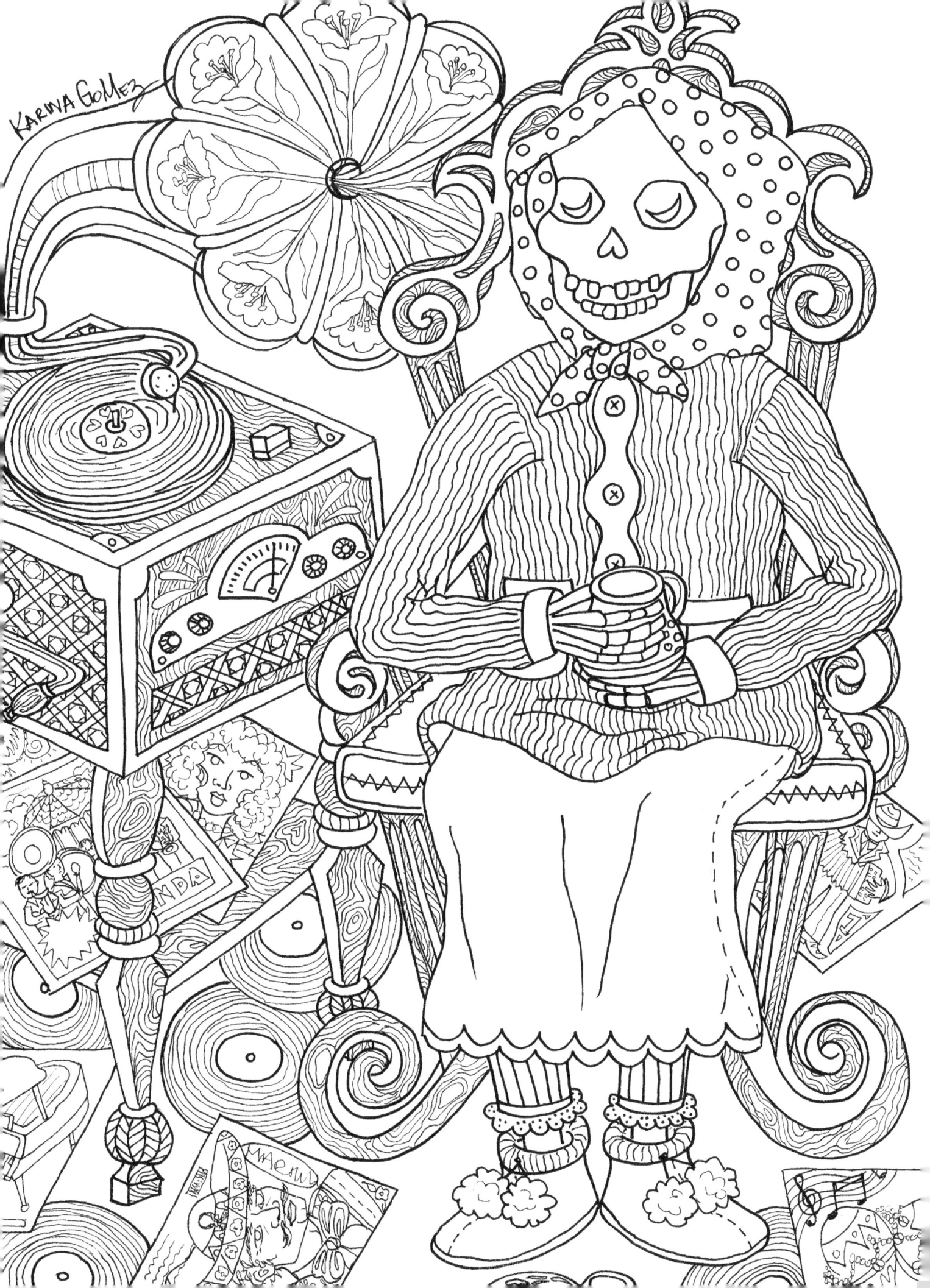

The children close their eyes
As a sweet serenade is played
Twinkling stars fill their dreams tonight
"Good night everyone!" they all say,
And thank the Lord for another day.

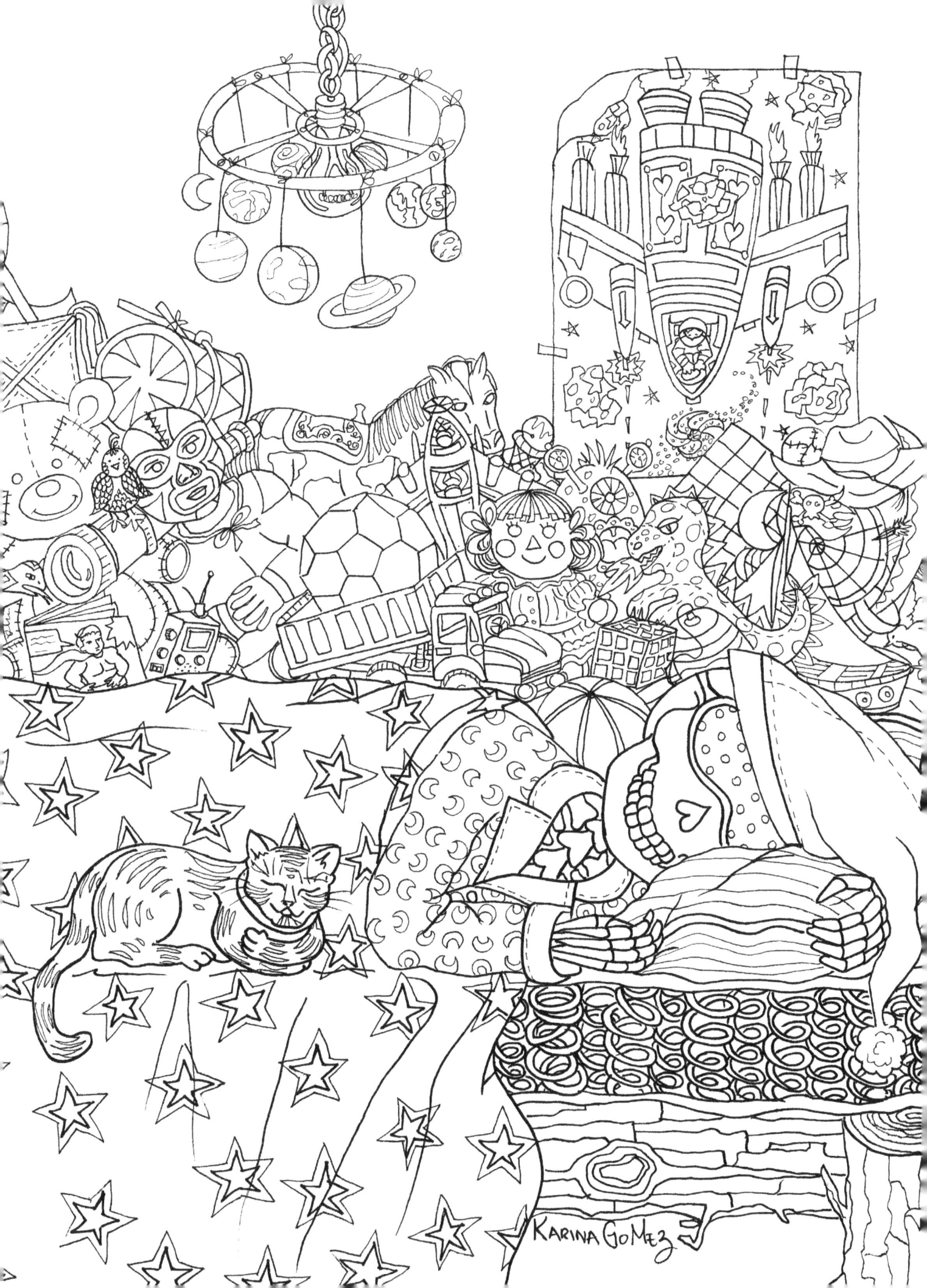

II

Dear Grandmother

Her love of life could be seen in her kitchen
That's where she whipped up her stews
And magically mixed in her spices

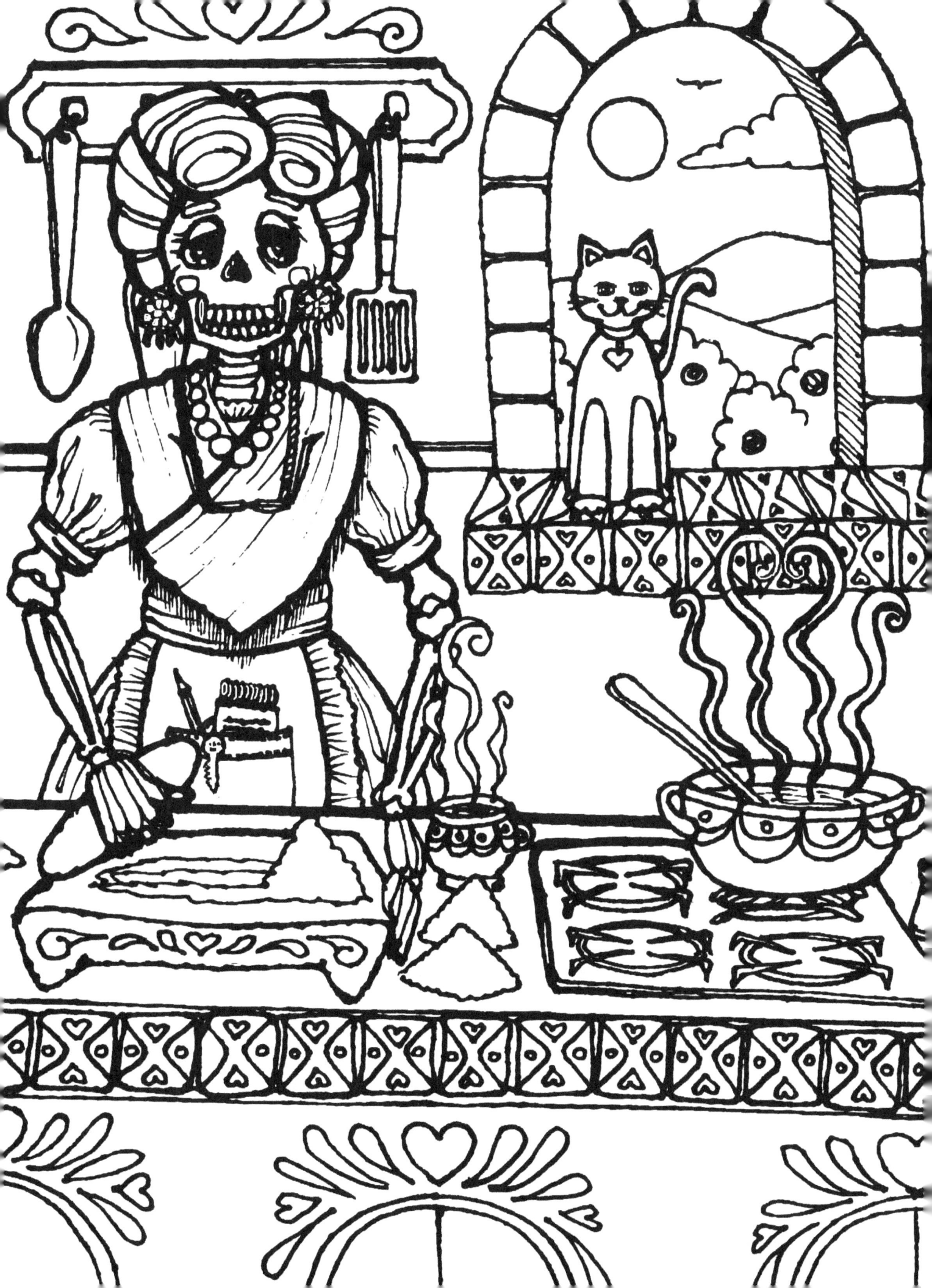

At times there was a cinnamon smell
That wafted through the air
And if you peered in the kitchen,
You would find her there

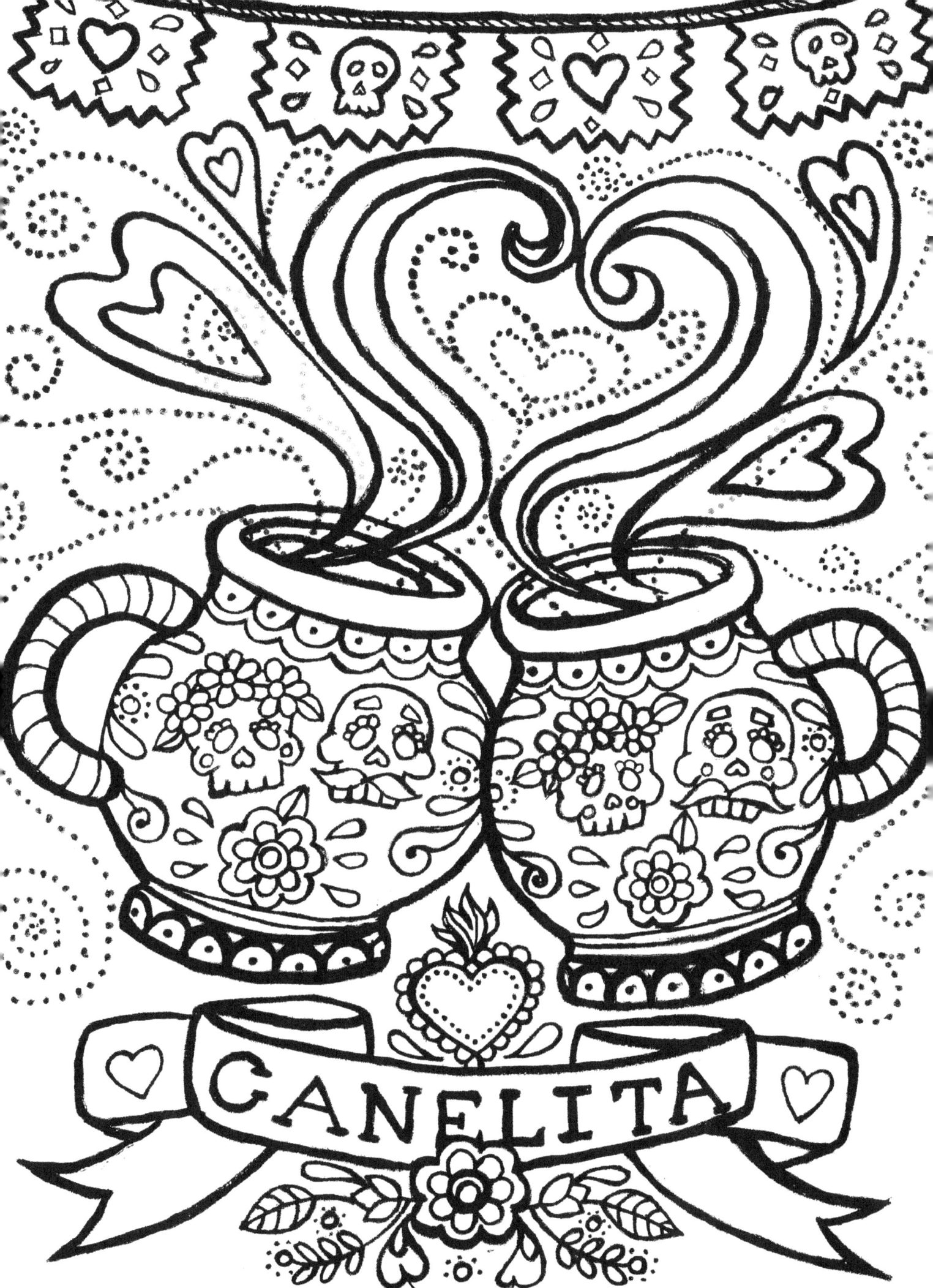

Grandmother, dear grandmother
Thank you for the love that you shared
It's because of these riches
That I'm fortunate to be your heir

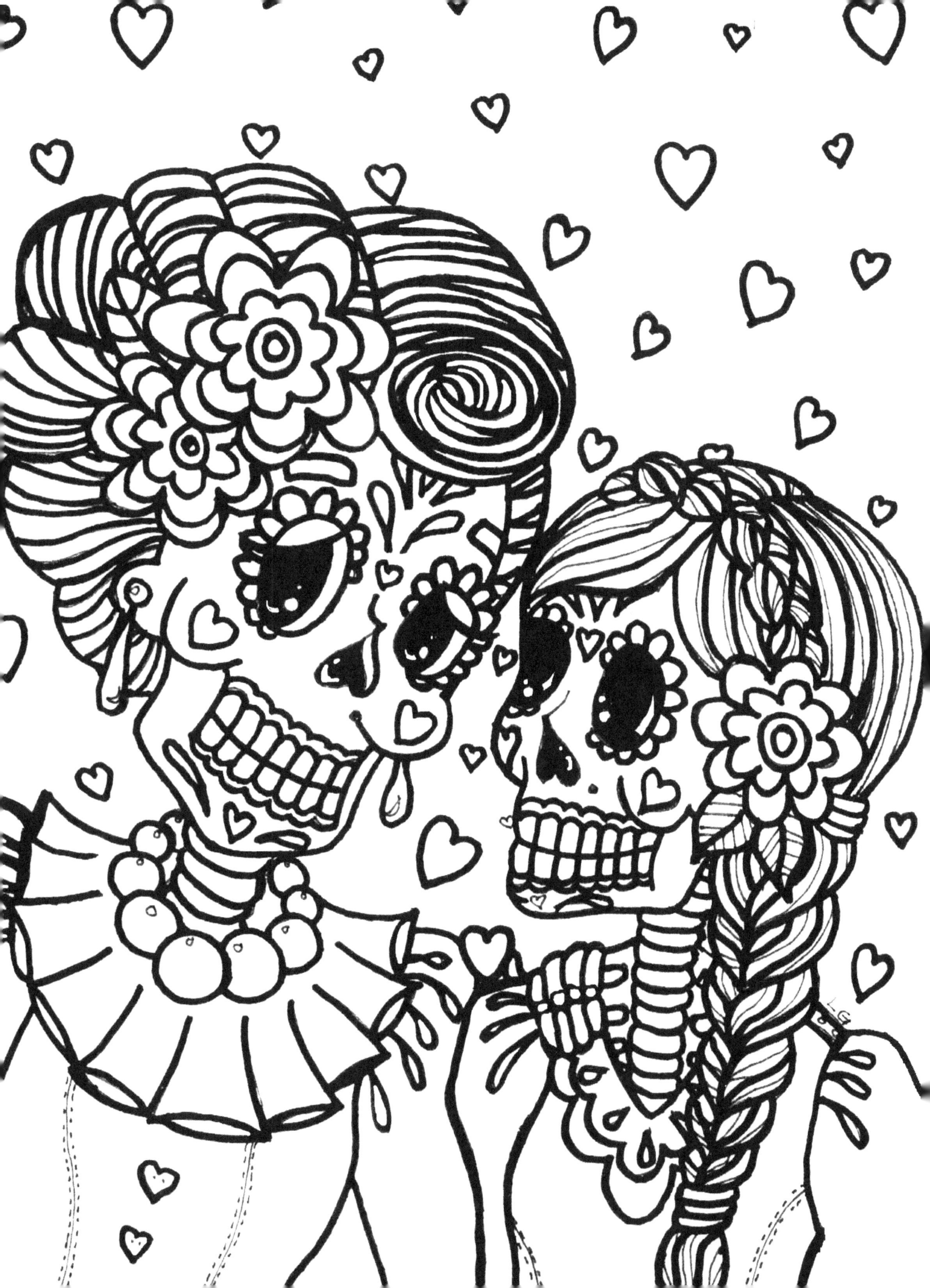

We will always cherish your lovely hands
With which you created with so much love
Those delicacies from your heart and soul
Always chased away the blues,
And were the perfect cure

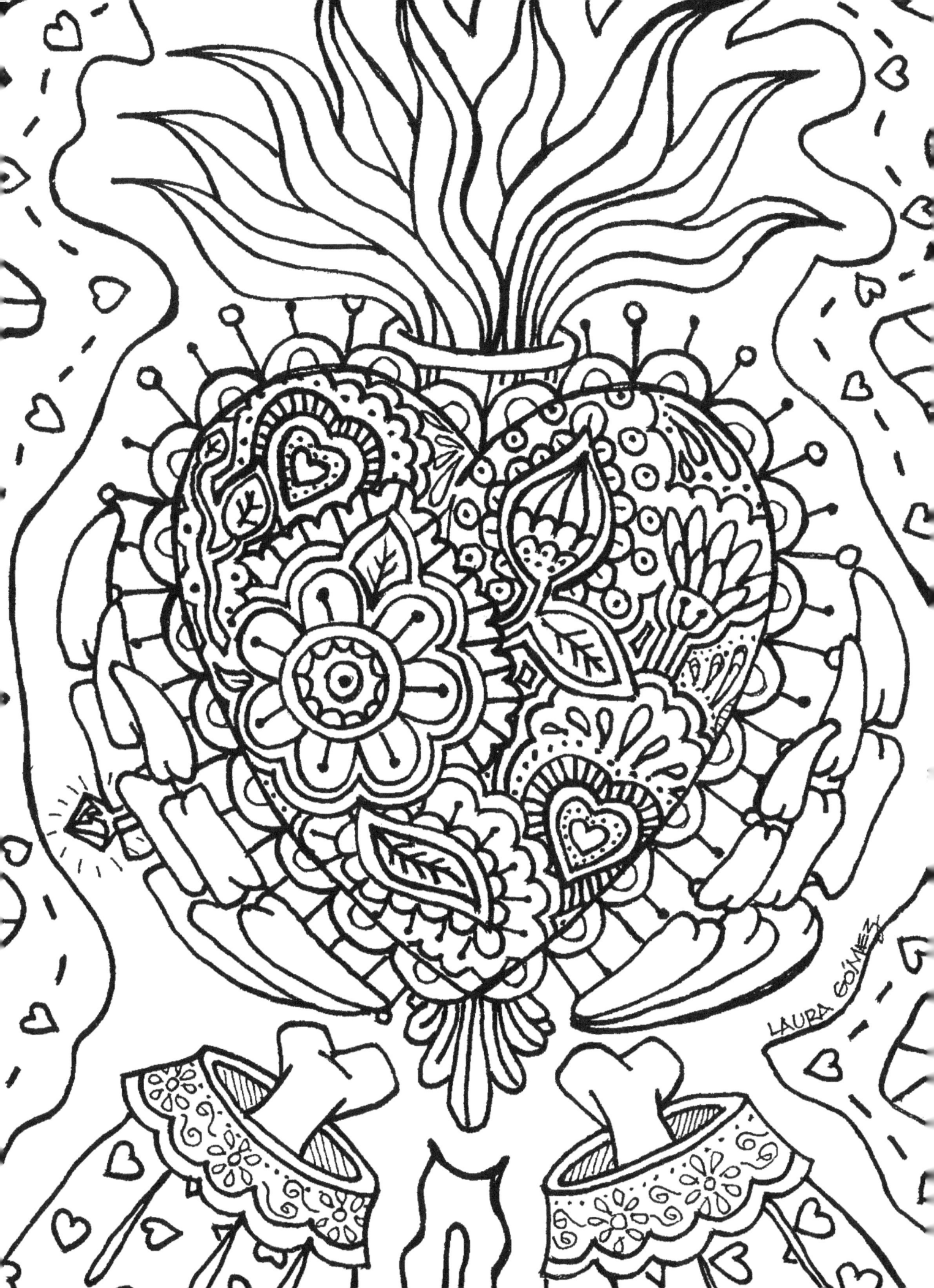

For all of these things and your tasty treats
We give our thanks to you
Grandmother, dear Grandmother

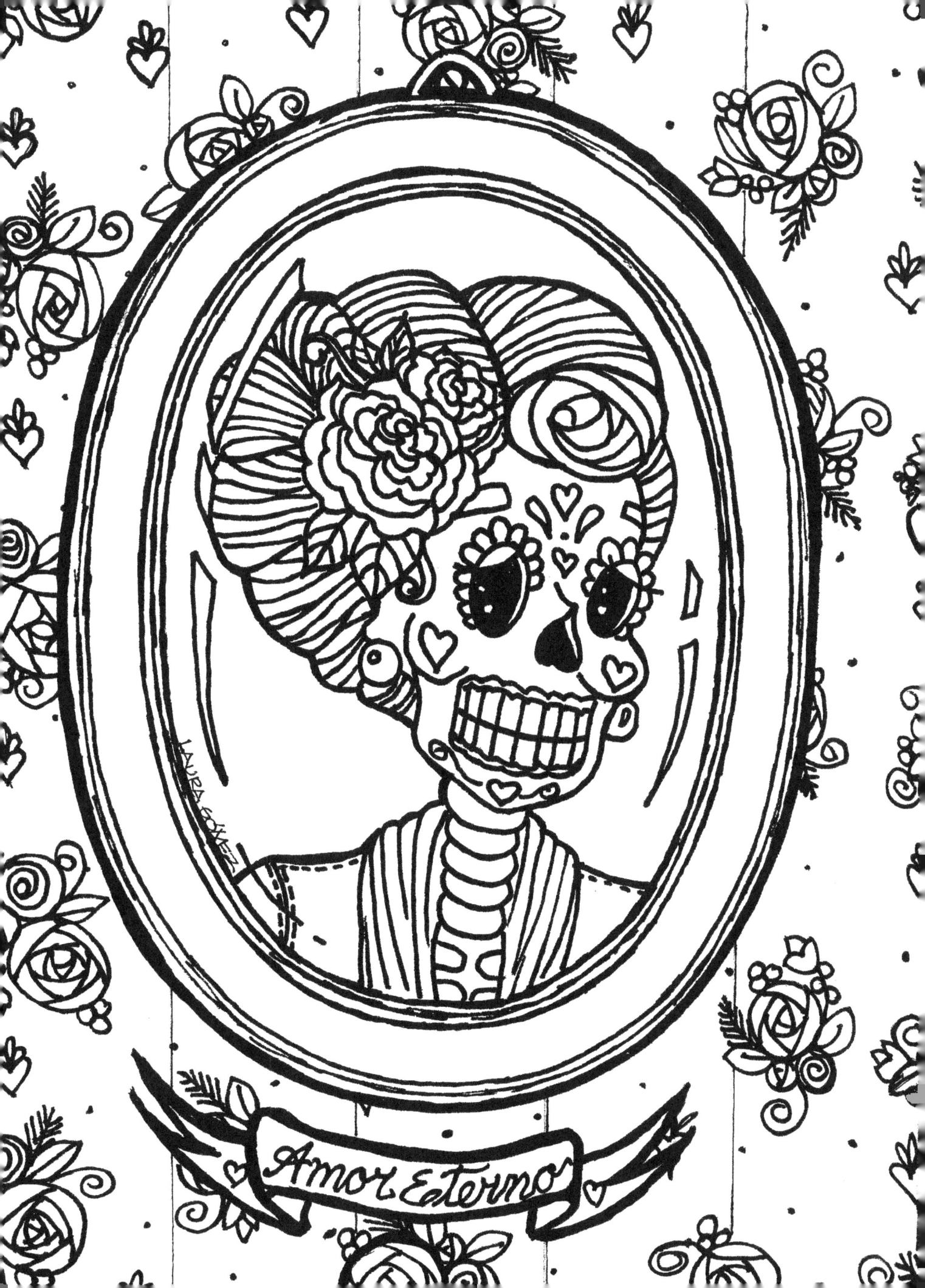

Amor Eterno

III

A Treasure: My Mother

The whole world over
Is looking for the love of their life

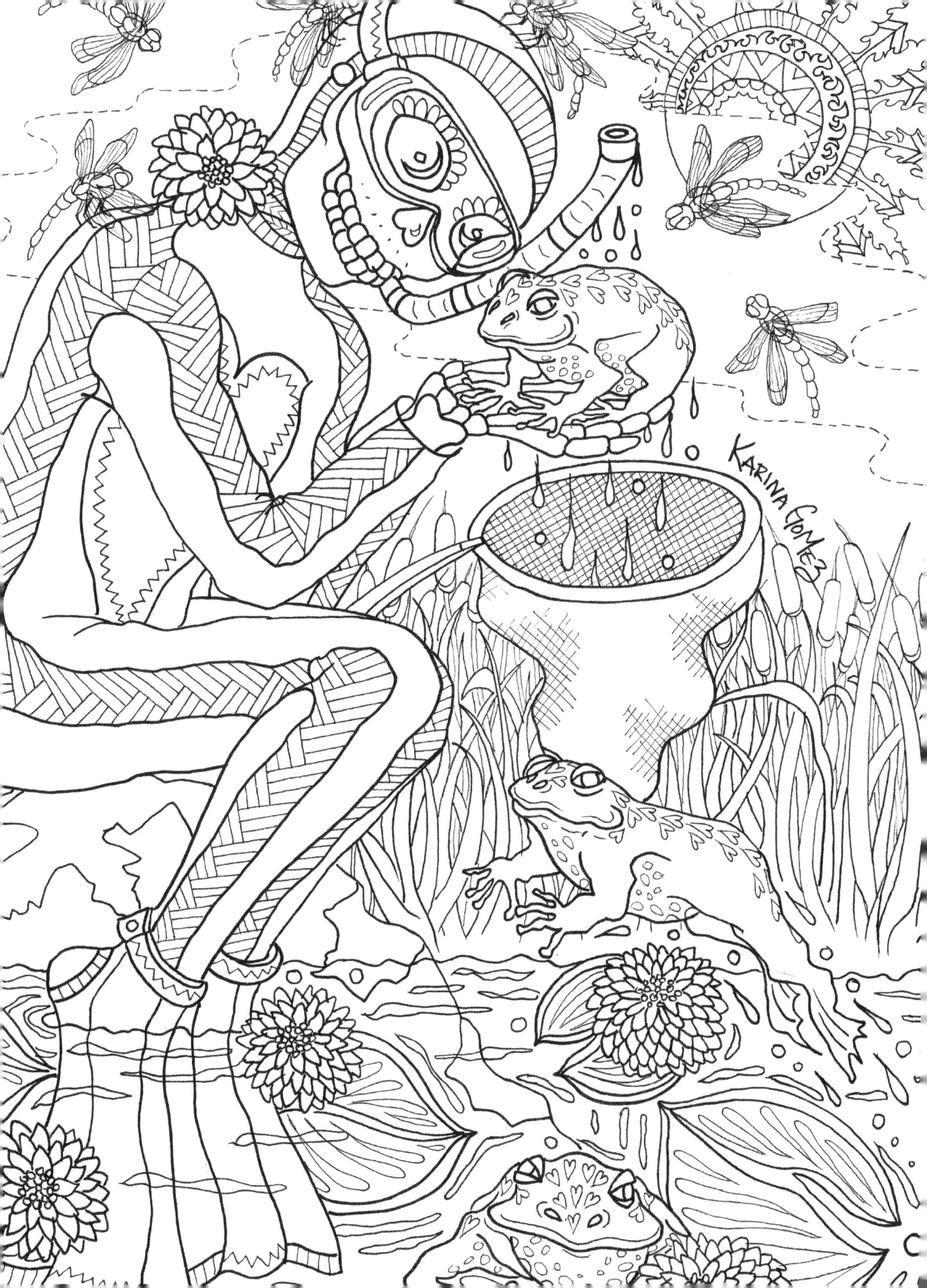

Some will scale mountains high
Others will swim stormy seas
Barely surviving treacherous waves
Only to be lost in the dark of night
Can anyone hear them?
Can anyone save them?

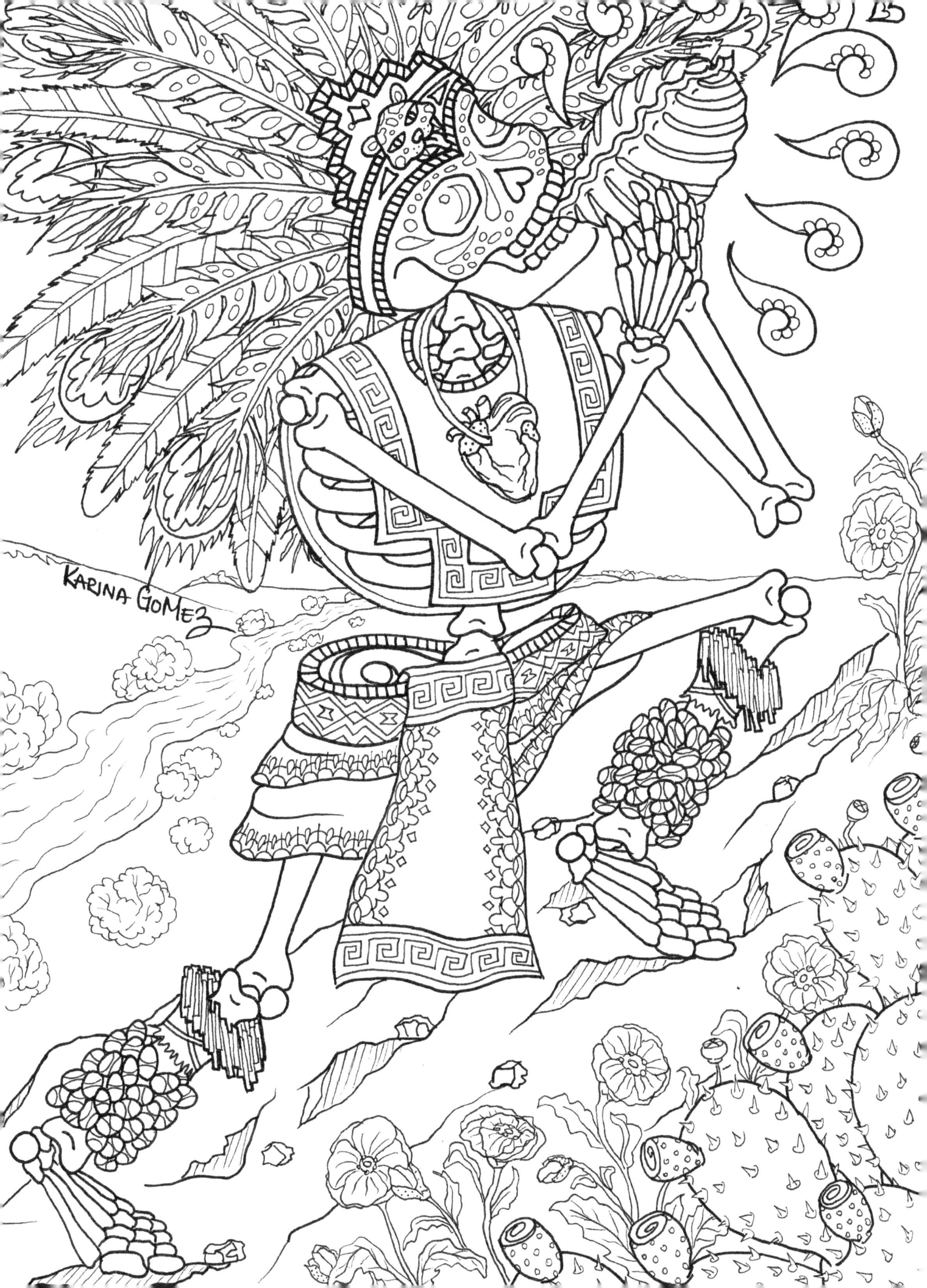

Their only hope is to find their way
Into the loving arms
Of their caring mom

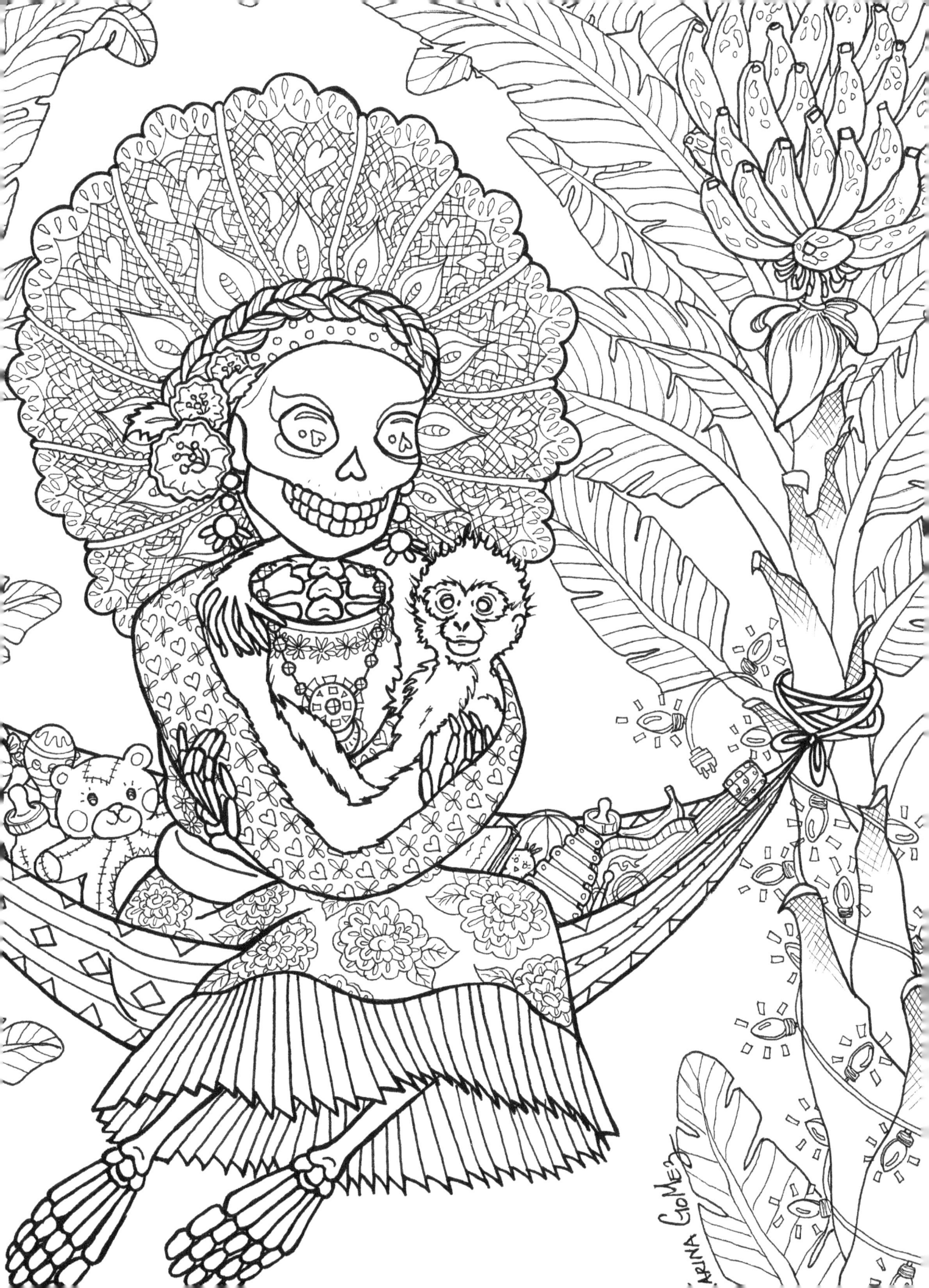

It's not silver
Not money, or even gold...

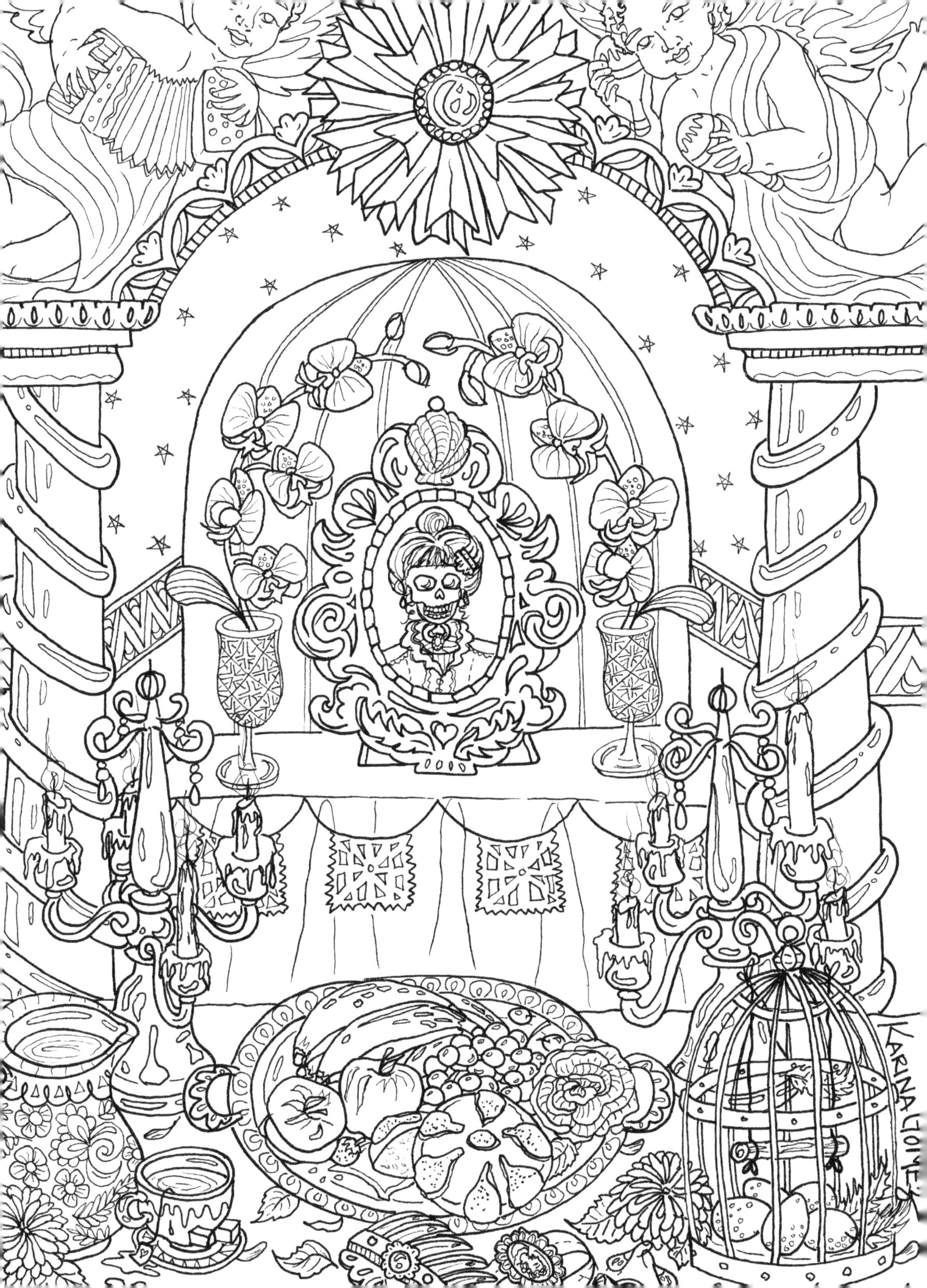

It is only my mother
Whom I adore.

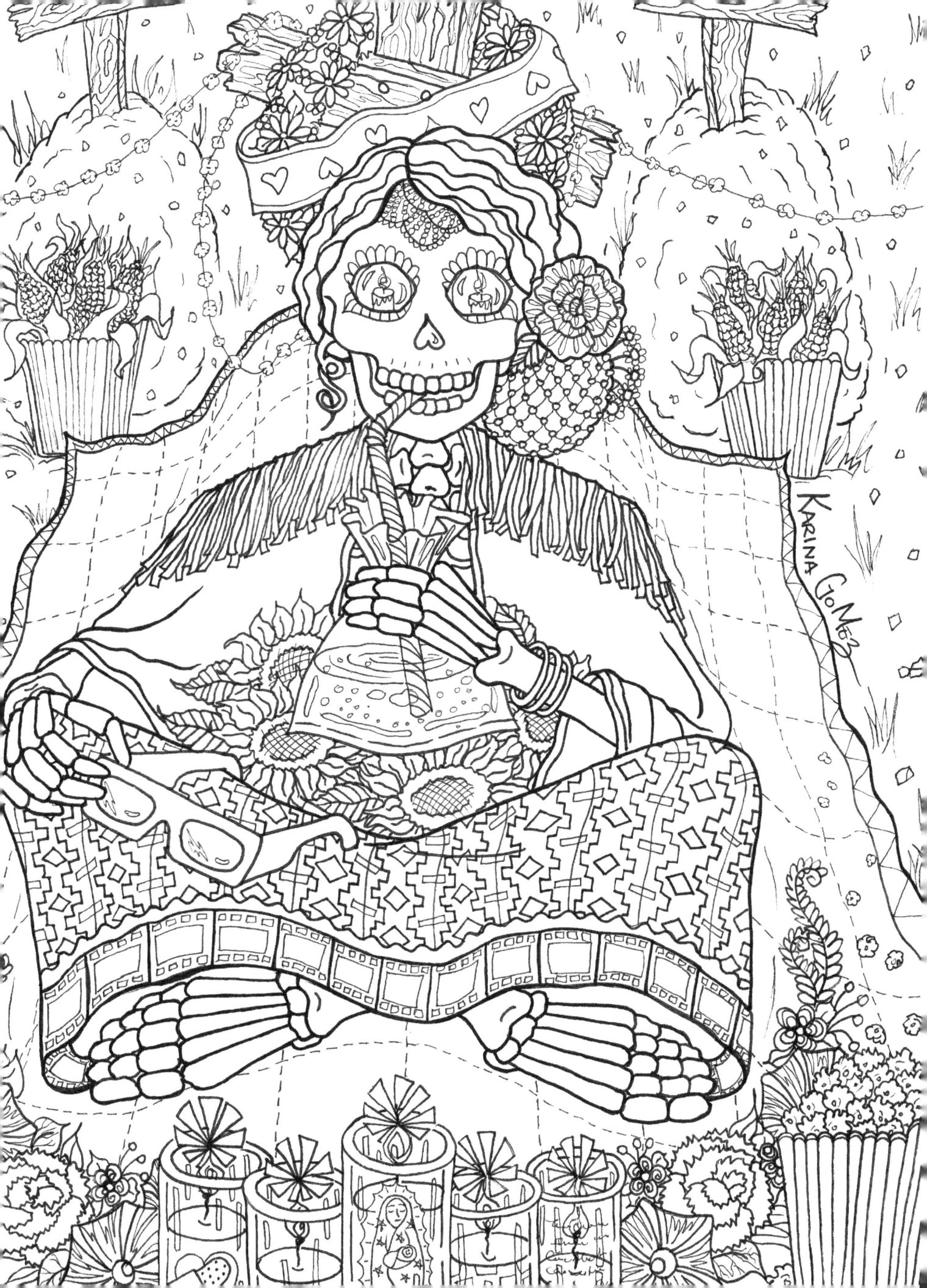

IV
Imagine a guitar

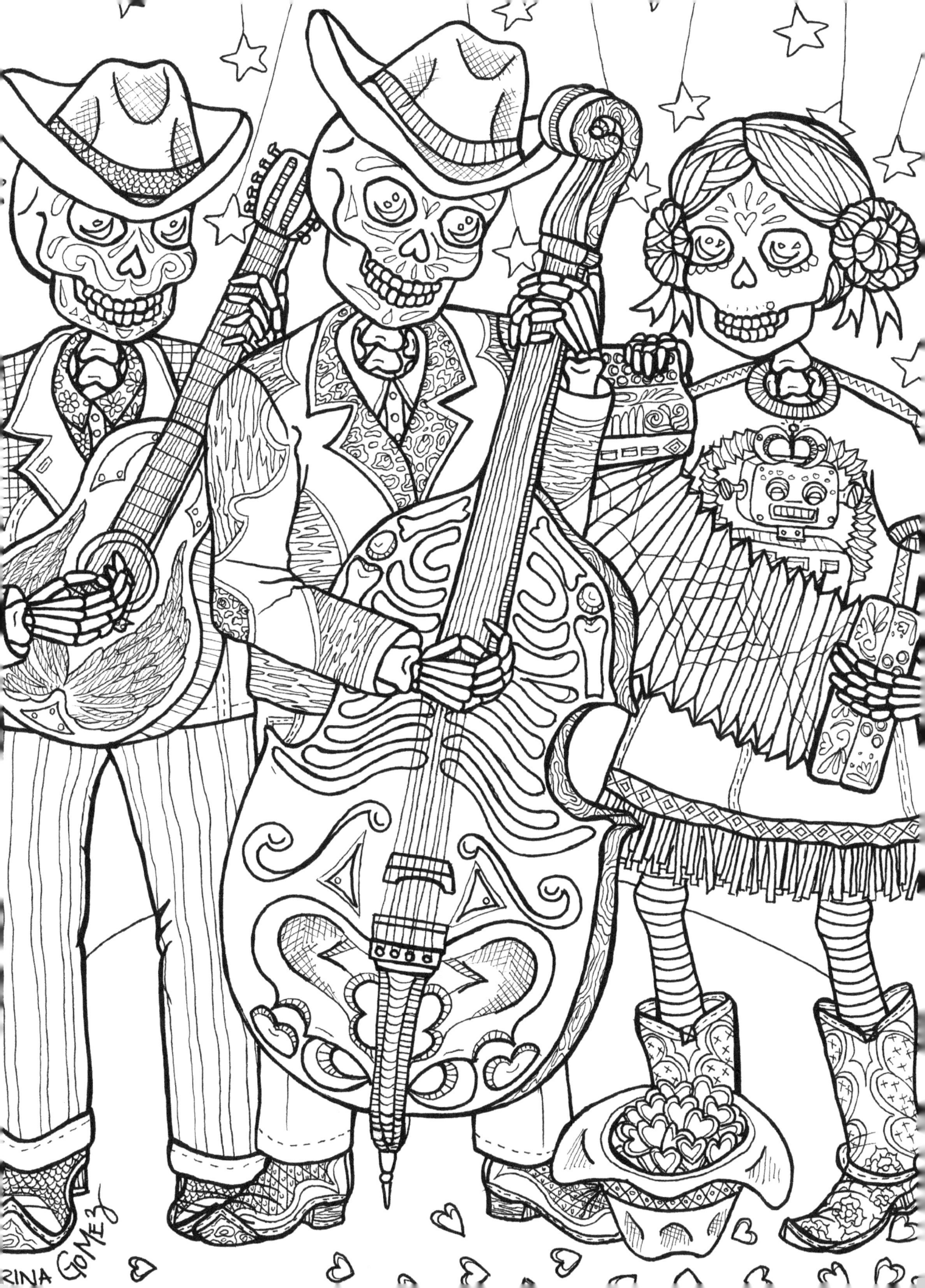

Take a moment to imagine a guitar
Its strings ringing
Resounding
Vibrating

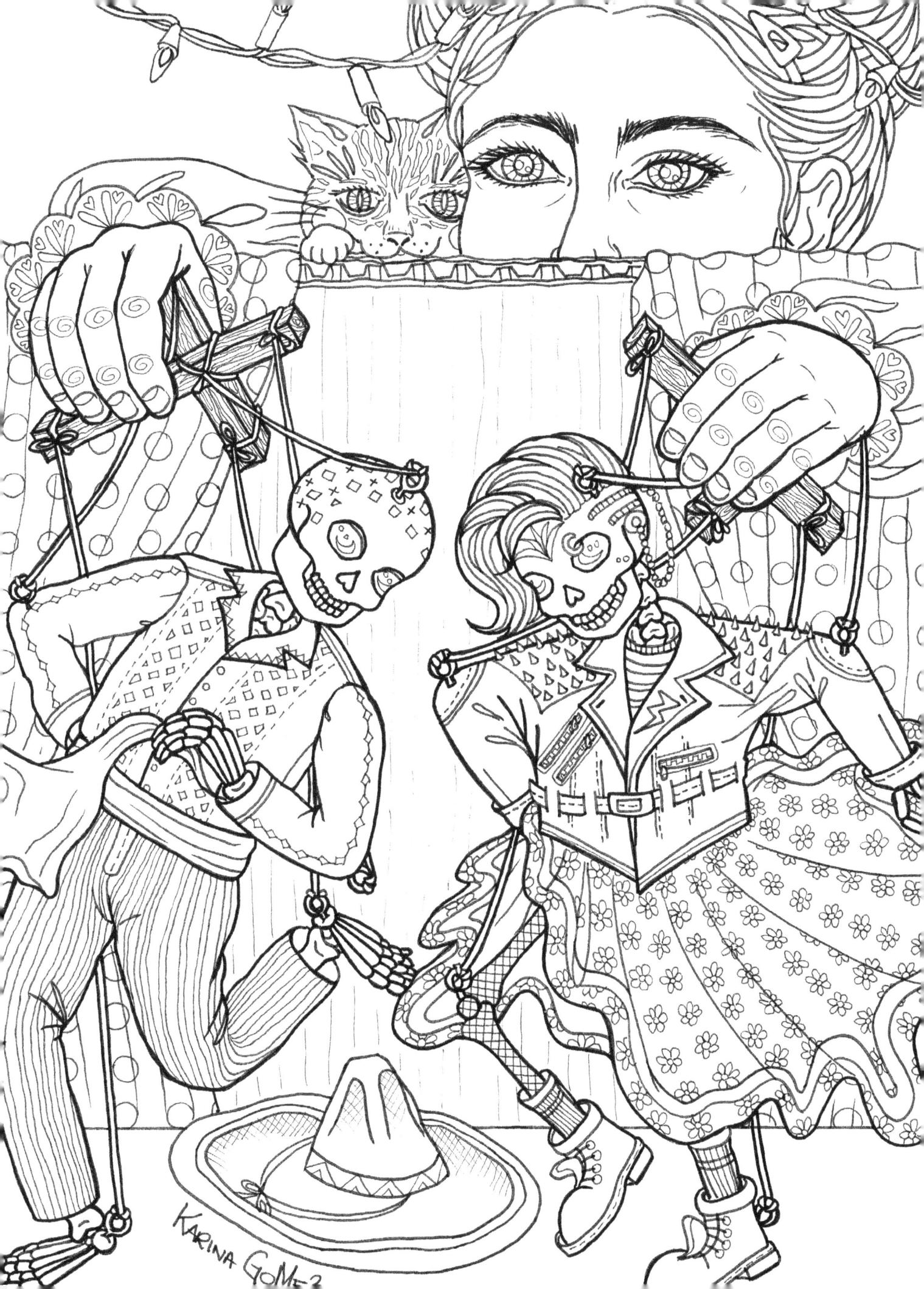

Each strum fills the space with notes
That emerge like bubble rainbows
And into butterflies magically transform

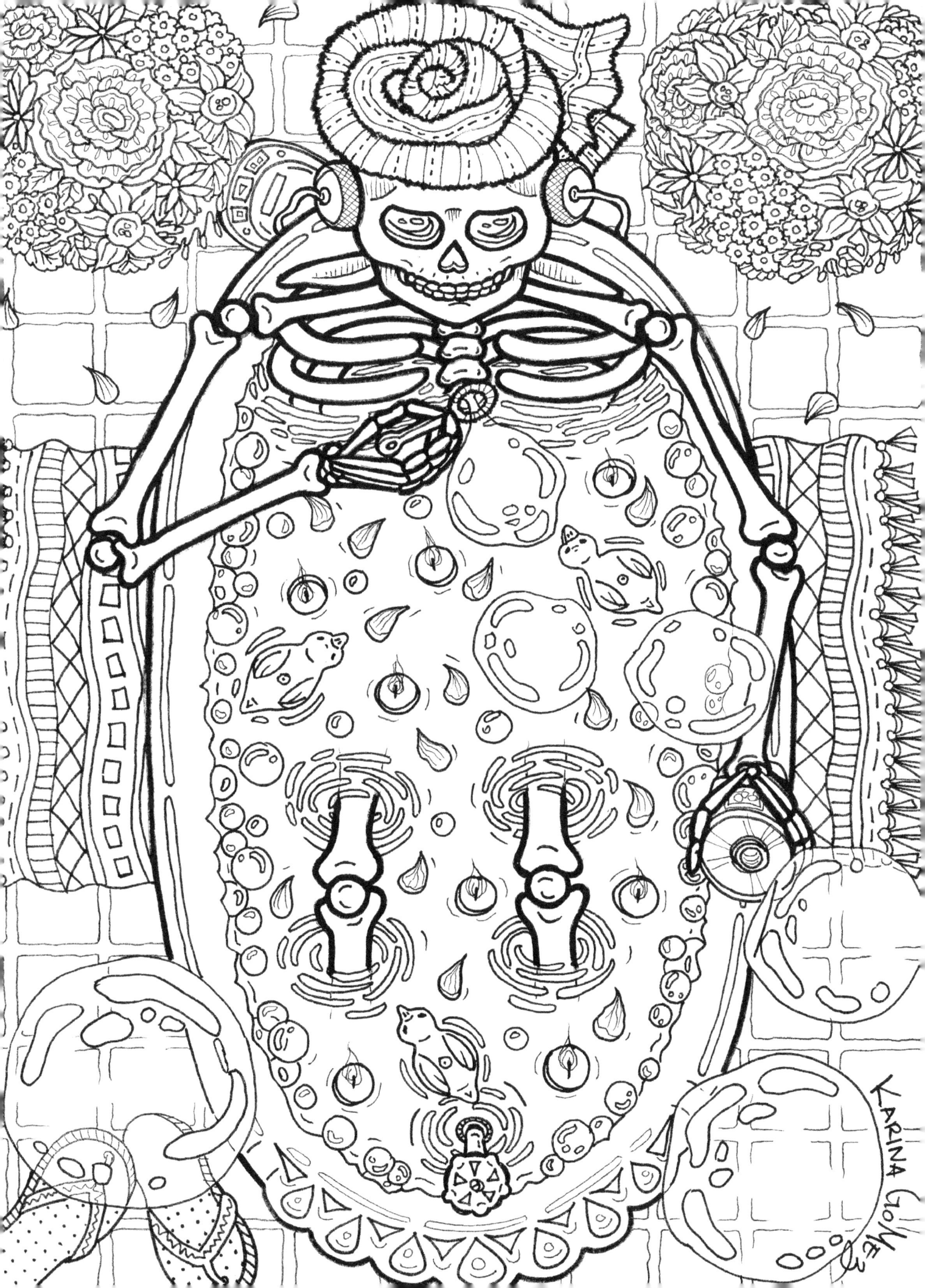

Some radiate blue
Others glow yellow

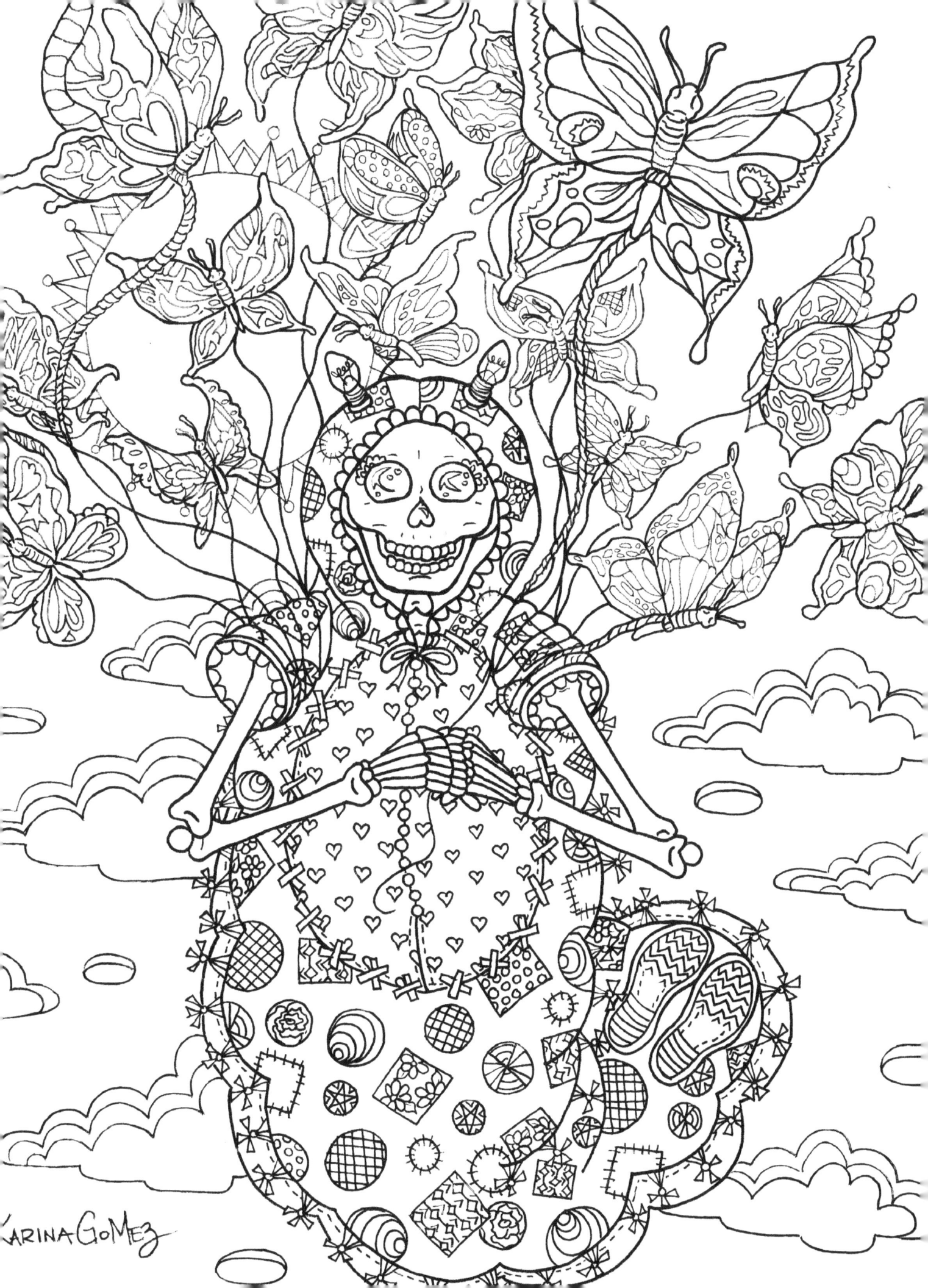

Some are burnt orange and velvety black
Trin Trin Trin
The strings giggle and laugh

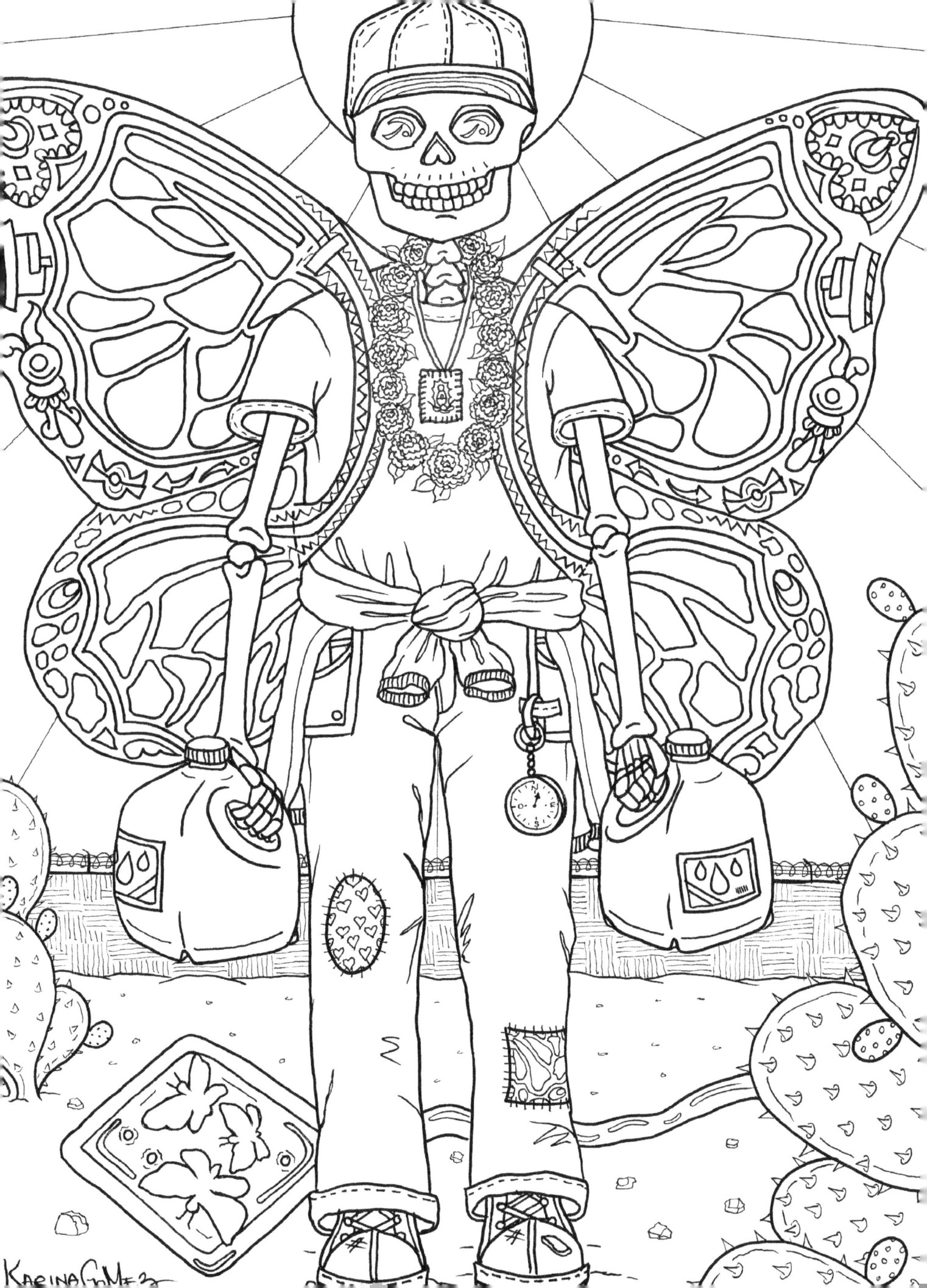

KaeinaGMF3

V

Our Daily Bread

Two young children gather kindling
They have been out looking since early mornin'
Like two little birds, they make a nest

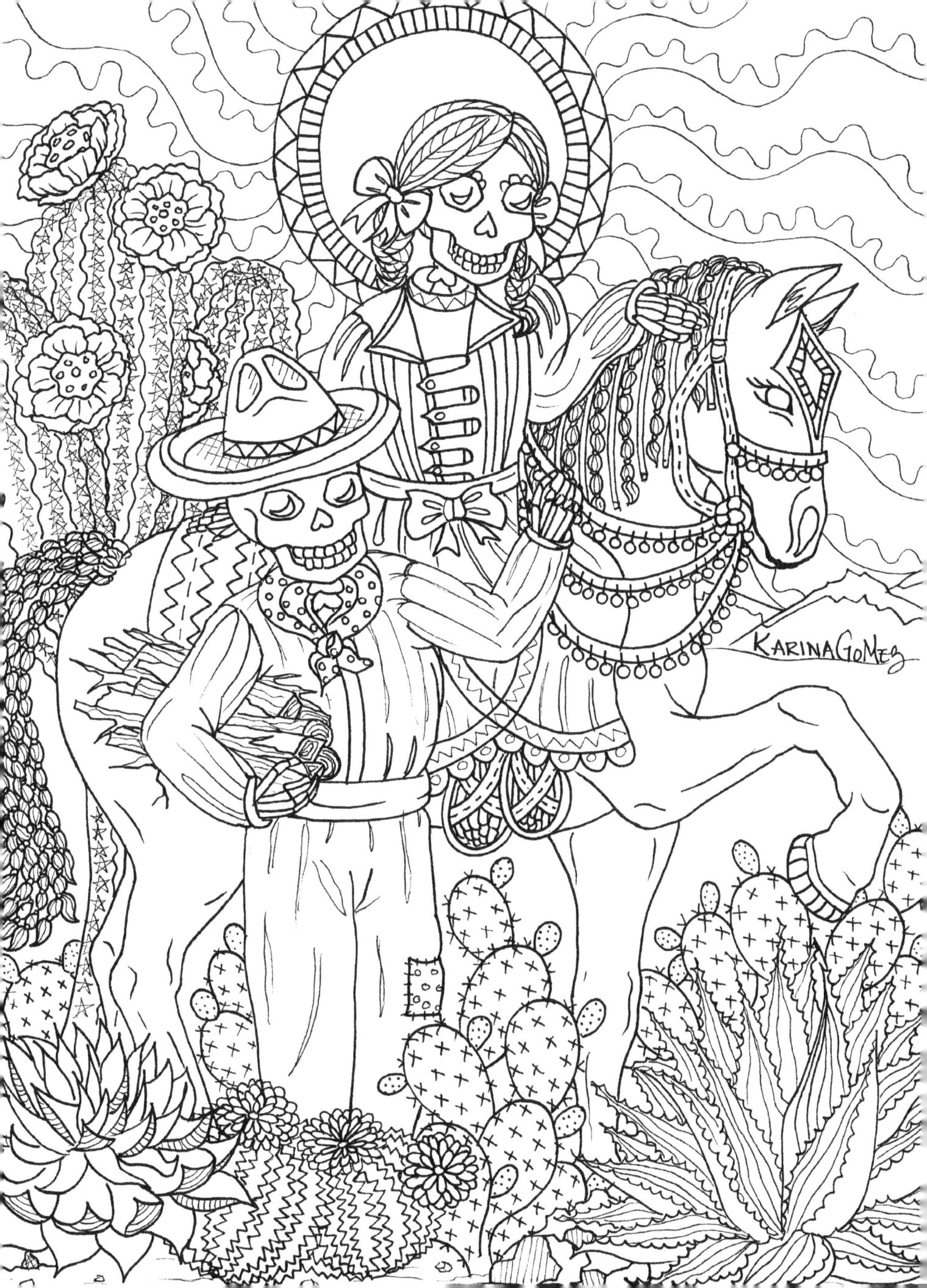

Mama is on her way back from the grindstone
What was once whole maize is now warm dough
The little nest of twigs is brought home

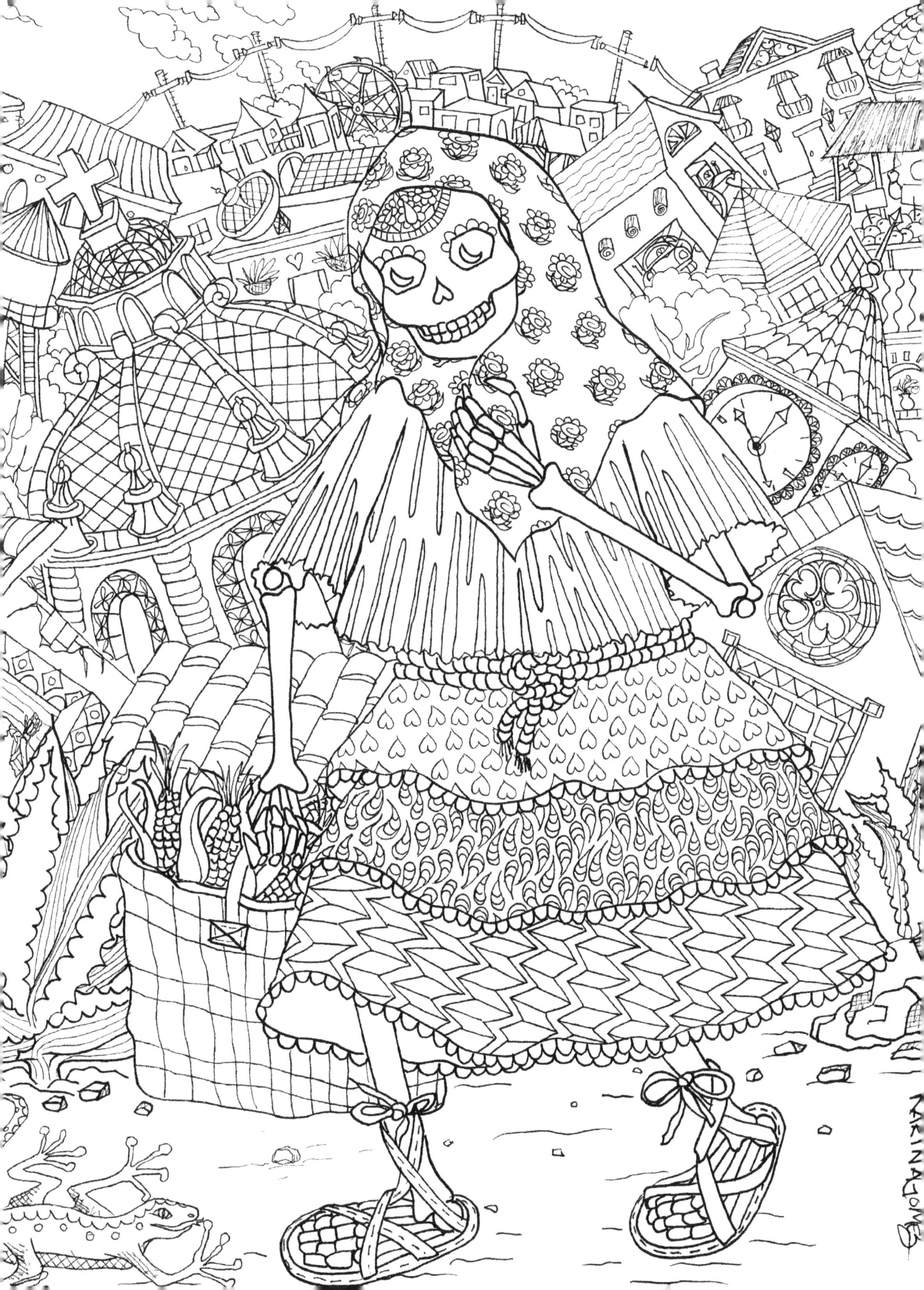

The pair of children play while dinner is done

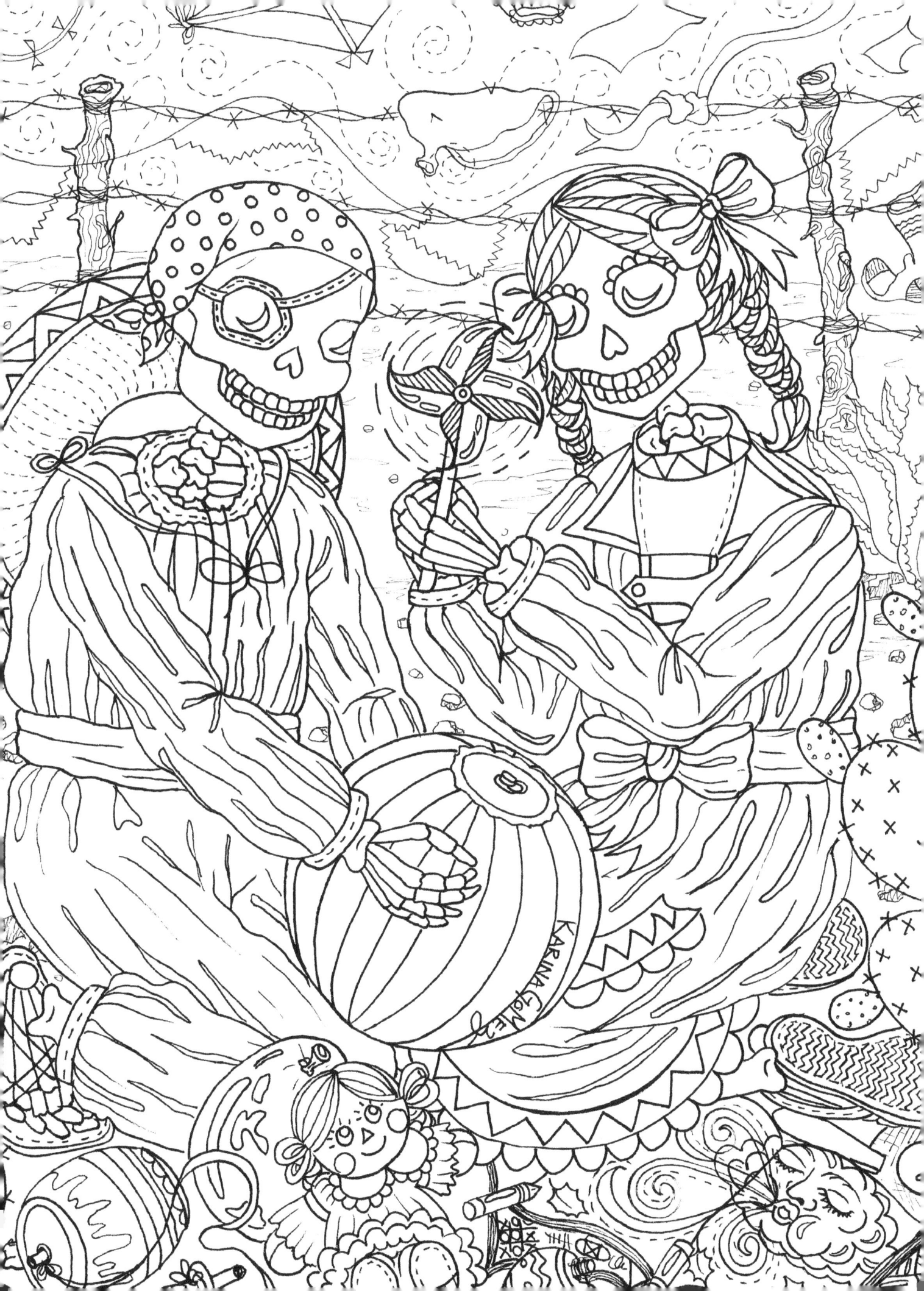

A potful of steamy beans
Simmer with succulent herbs

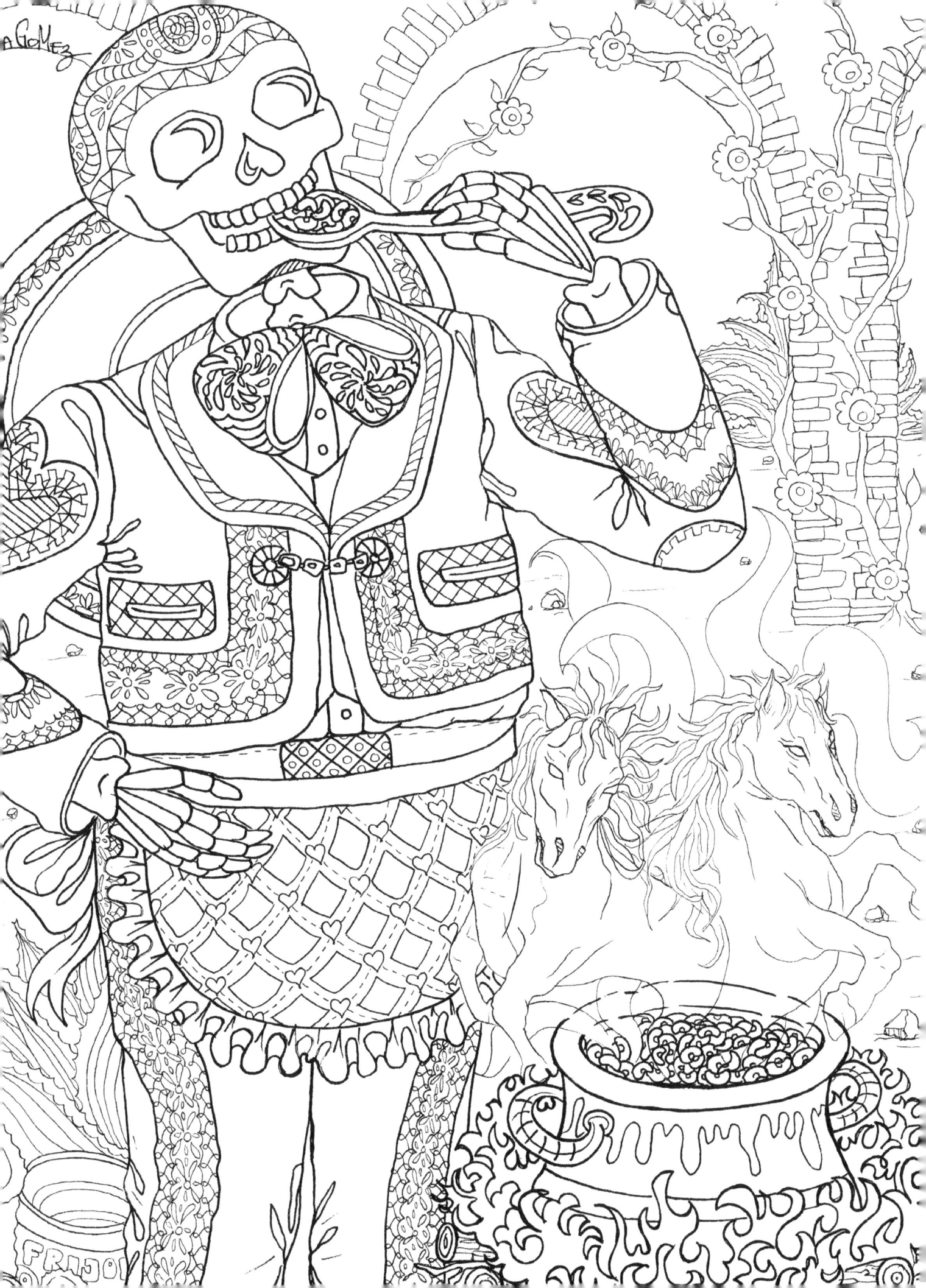

As if by magic, it appears on the table
The vapor clears
The tasty aroma kisses the air

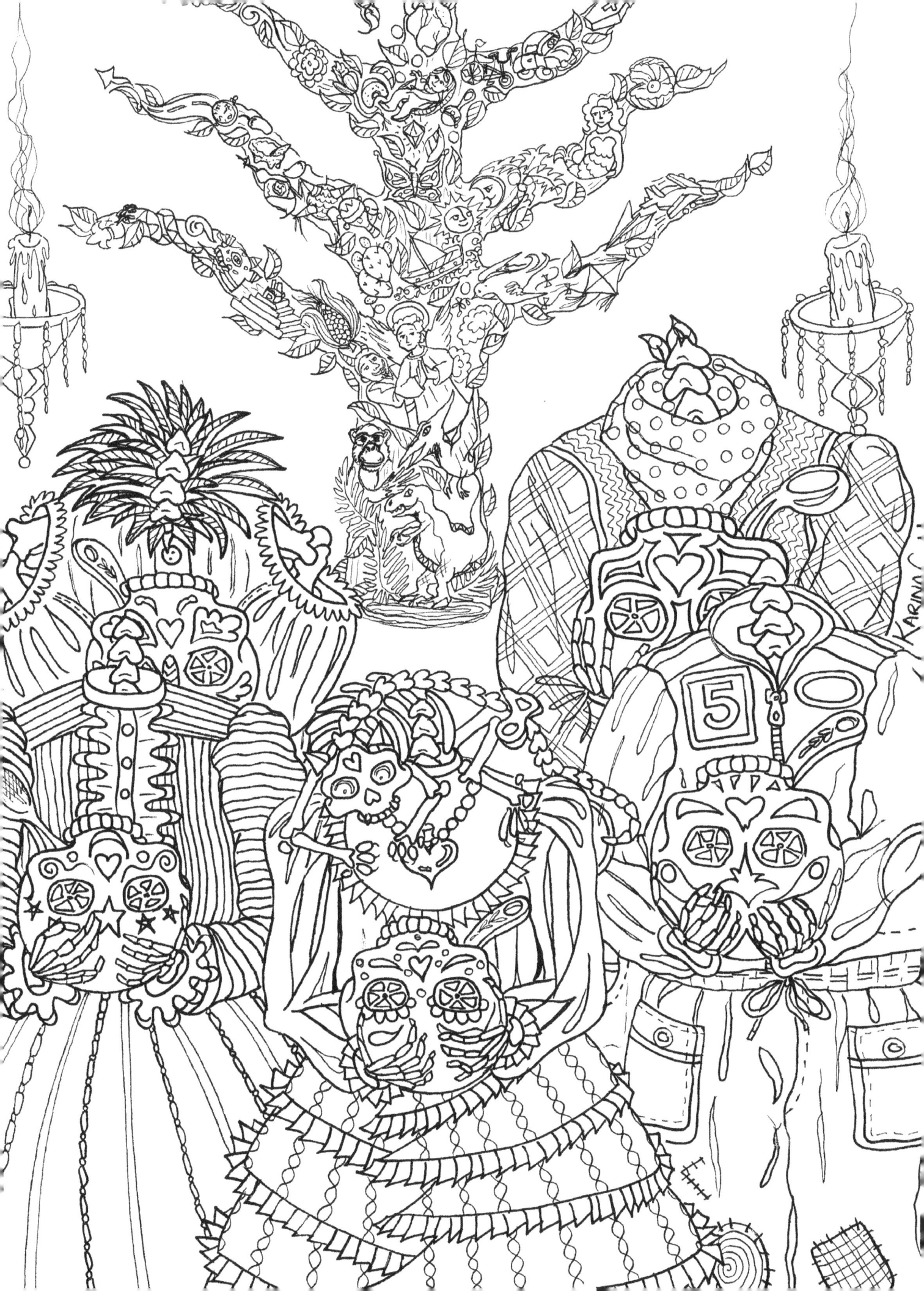

VI
The Valley

The day is dressed up for summer fun
A tortilla sun sizzles in the sky
Water hoses splash wildly around
Cooling off the morning sun

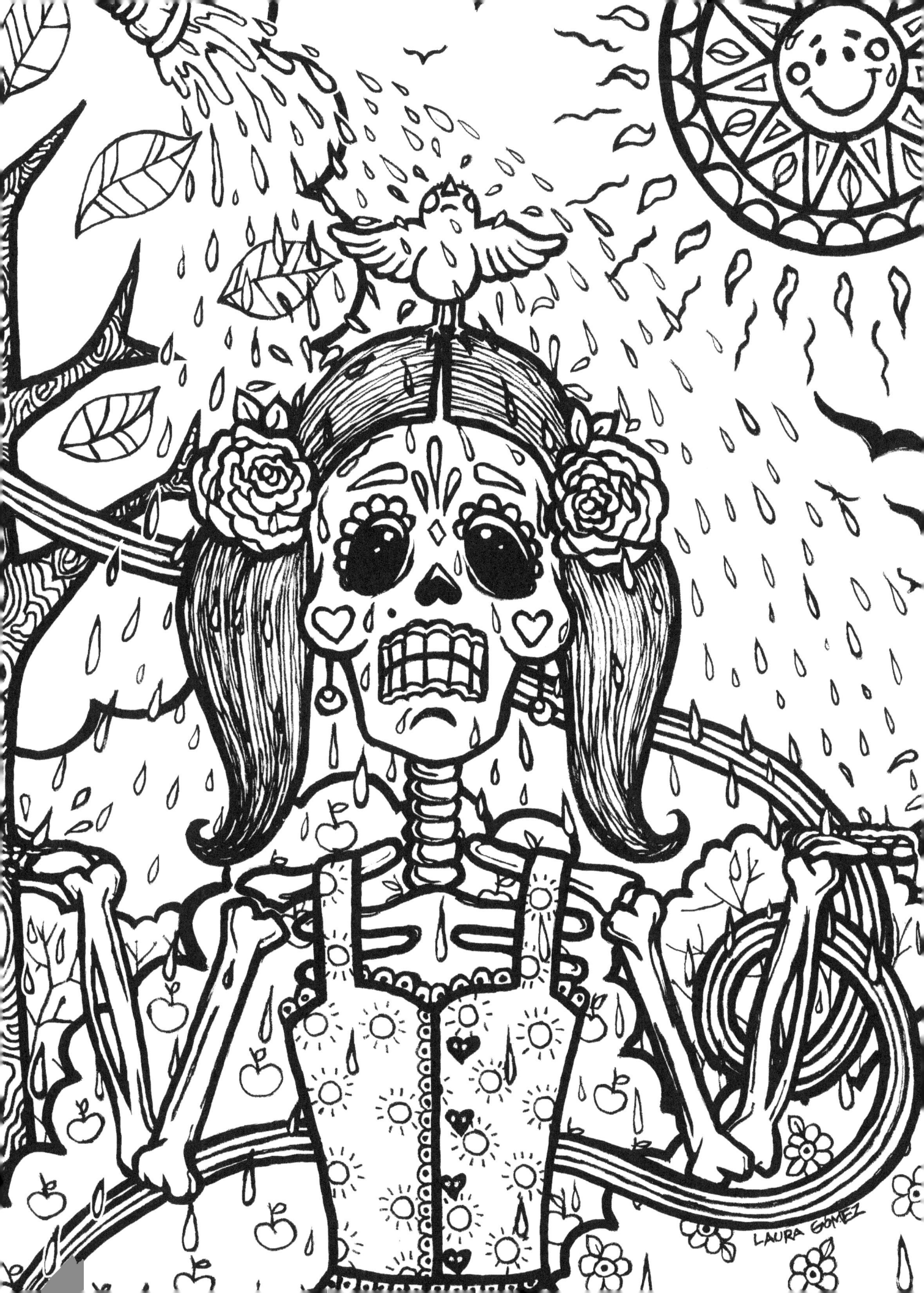

LAURA GOMEZ

A little one cries but no one minds
Since moms take time to catch up and talk,
"You don't say?," they chit-chat along.
Soon, it's good-bye as their feet flippity flop away
Everyone back in their own little houses again

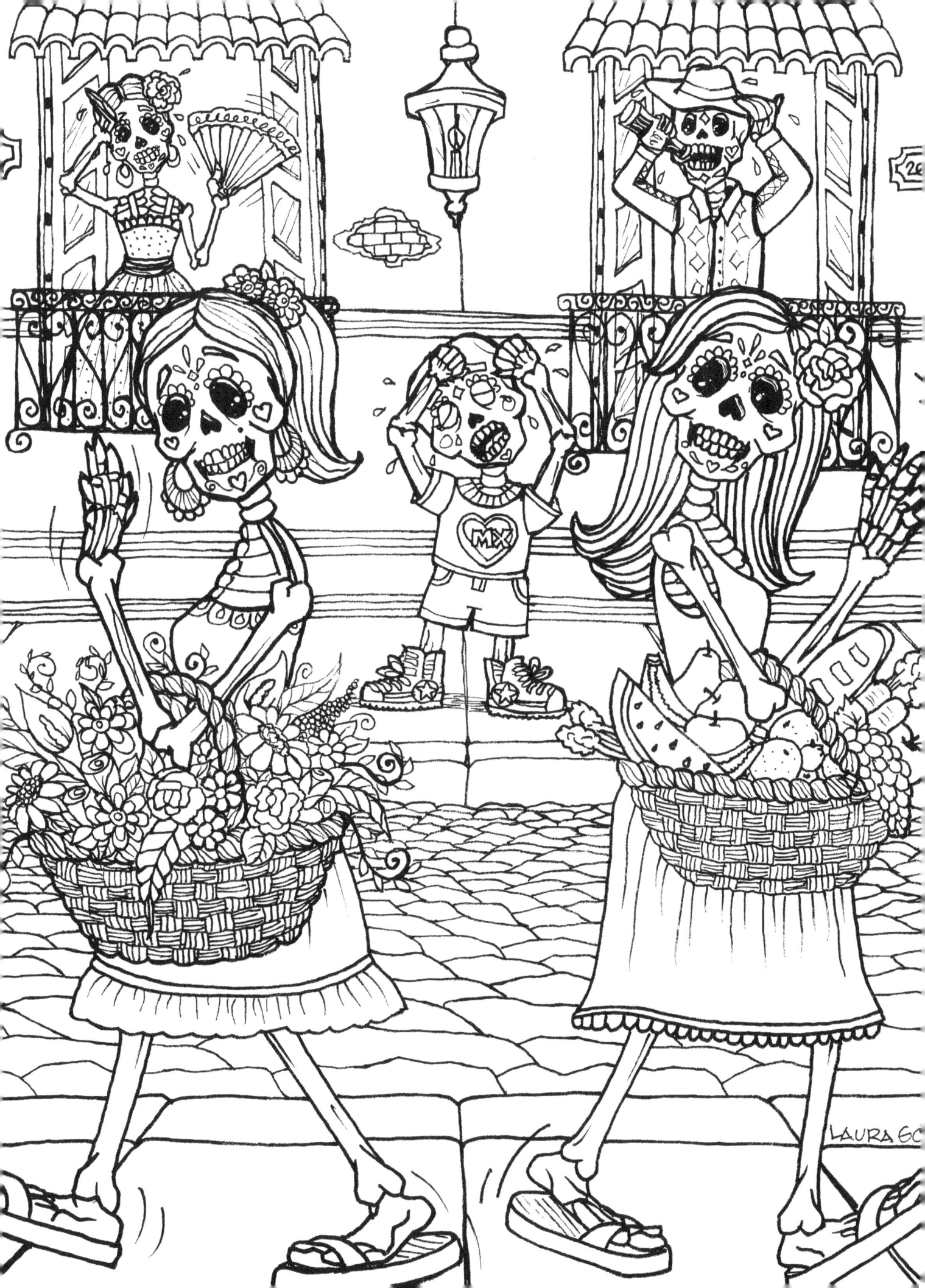

Hand-tossed tortillas are made
Rolled inside, refried beans
and fried potatoes are warm
And later, the plates and cups
Bob and dance in the suds

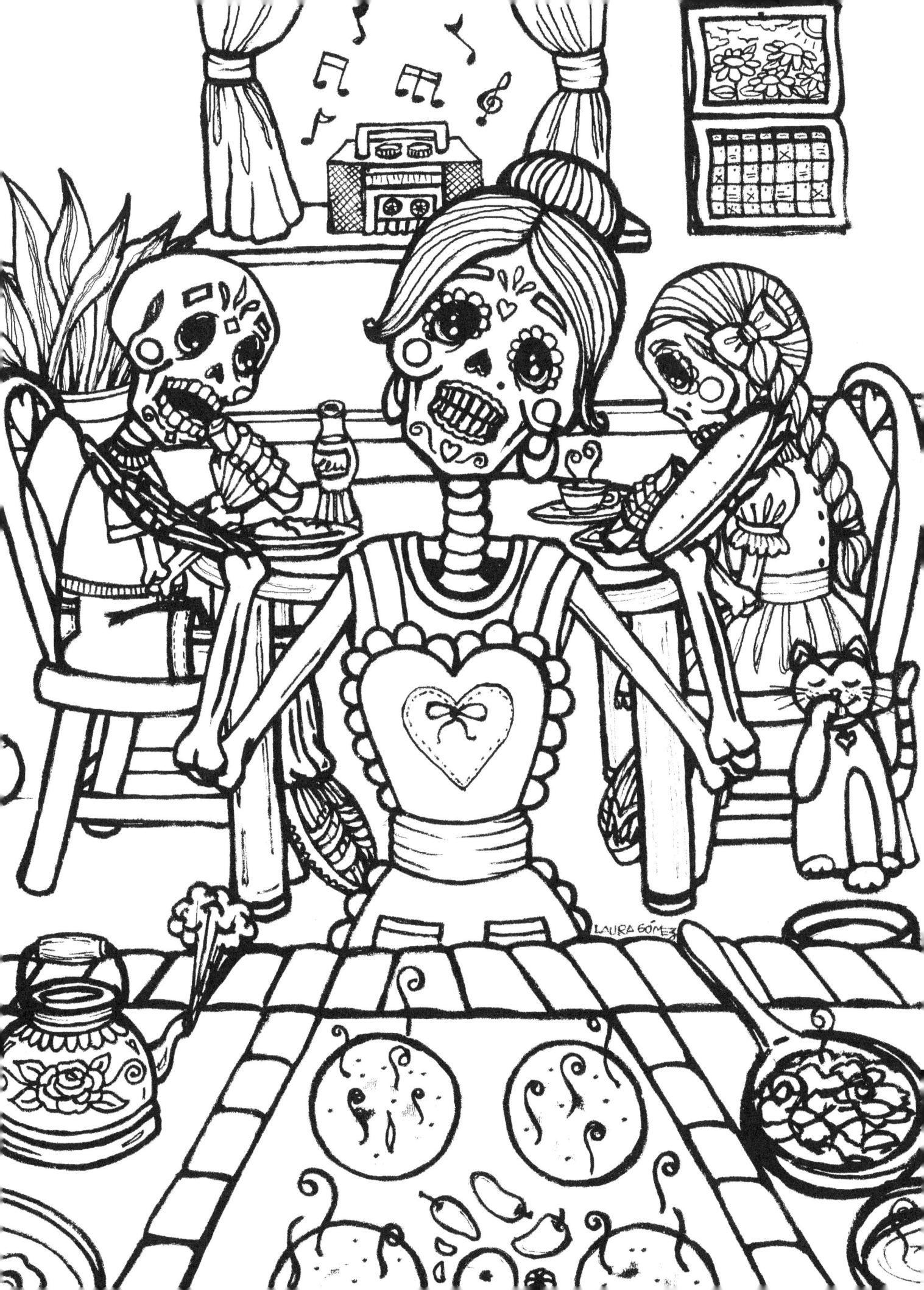

Silence falls and with it a peacefulness, too
Every minute runs into the night
Crickets invade the hot, stiff air
Sirens in the distance woefully wail

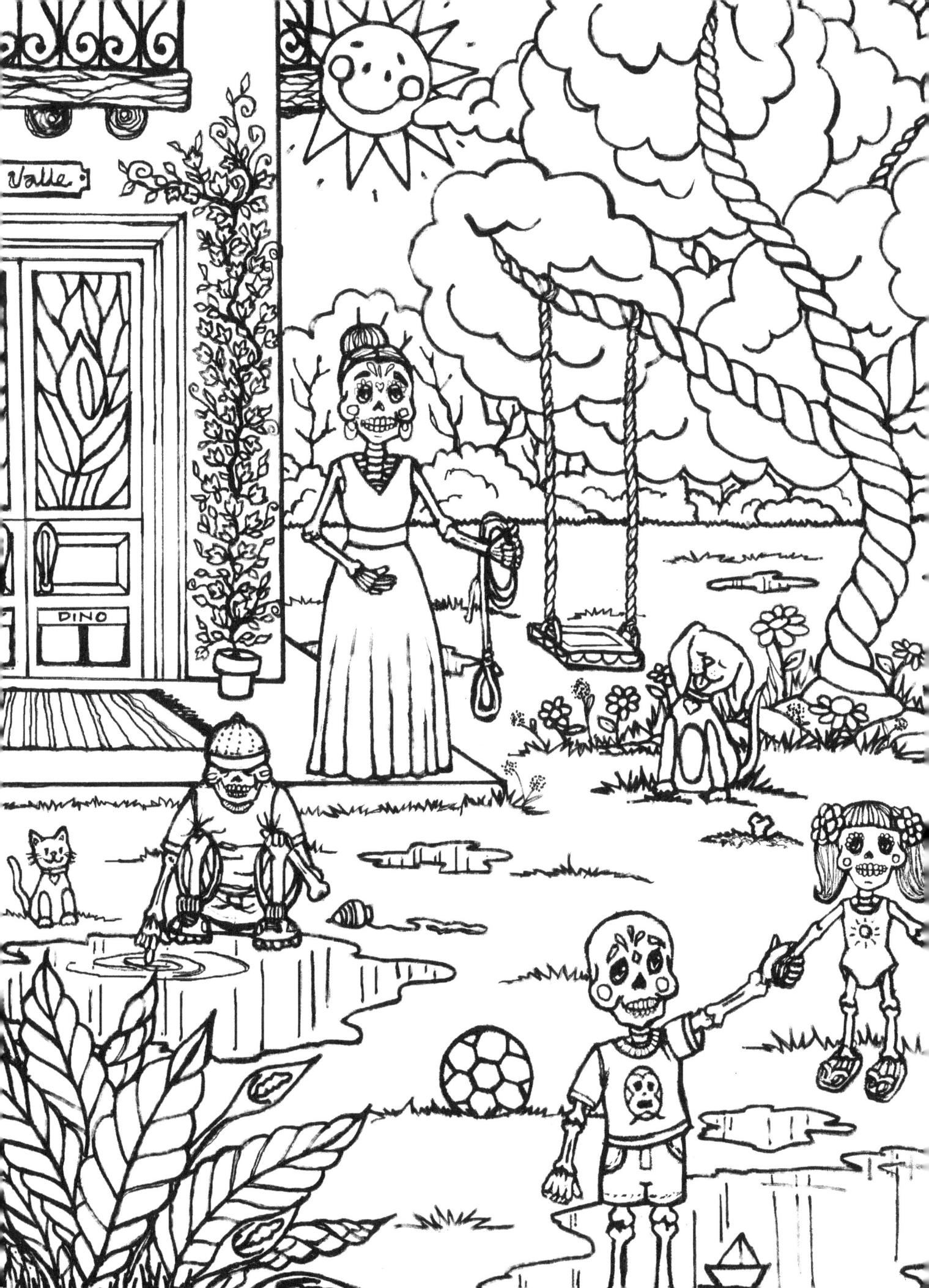

Not even the night sky can quash the heat
Instead, with a fury, it seems to increase
Eyelids fall heavy and drop like curtains
The crickets' song ends
And finally, sleep wins

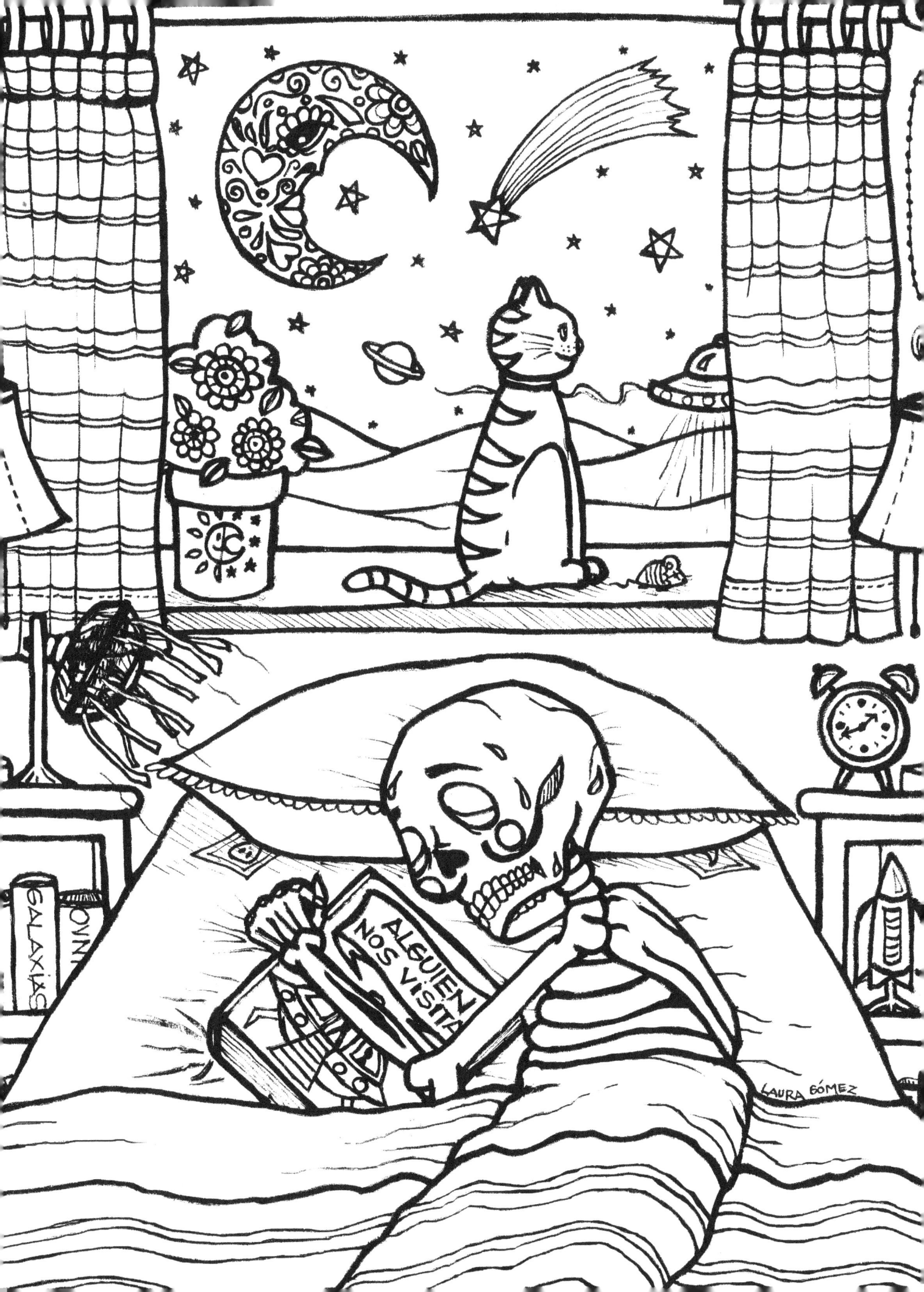

VII
Sweet Freedom

As a child, I was happy, carefree
I carried in my heart a steady beat
My feet traipsed along with an unstoppable cadence
One day I followed a little bird through the trees
Imitating its voice, to see if I could sing

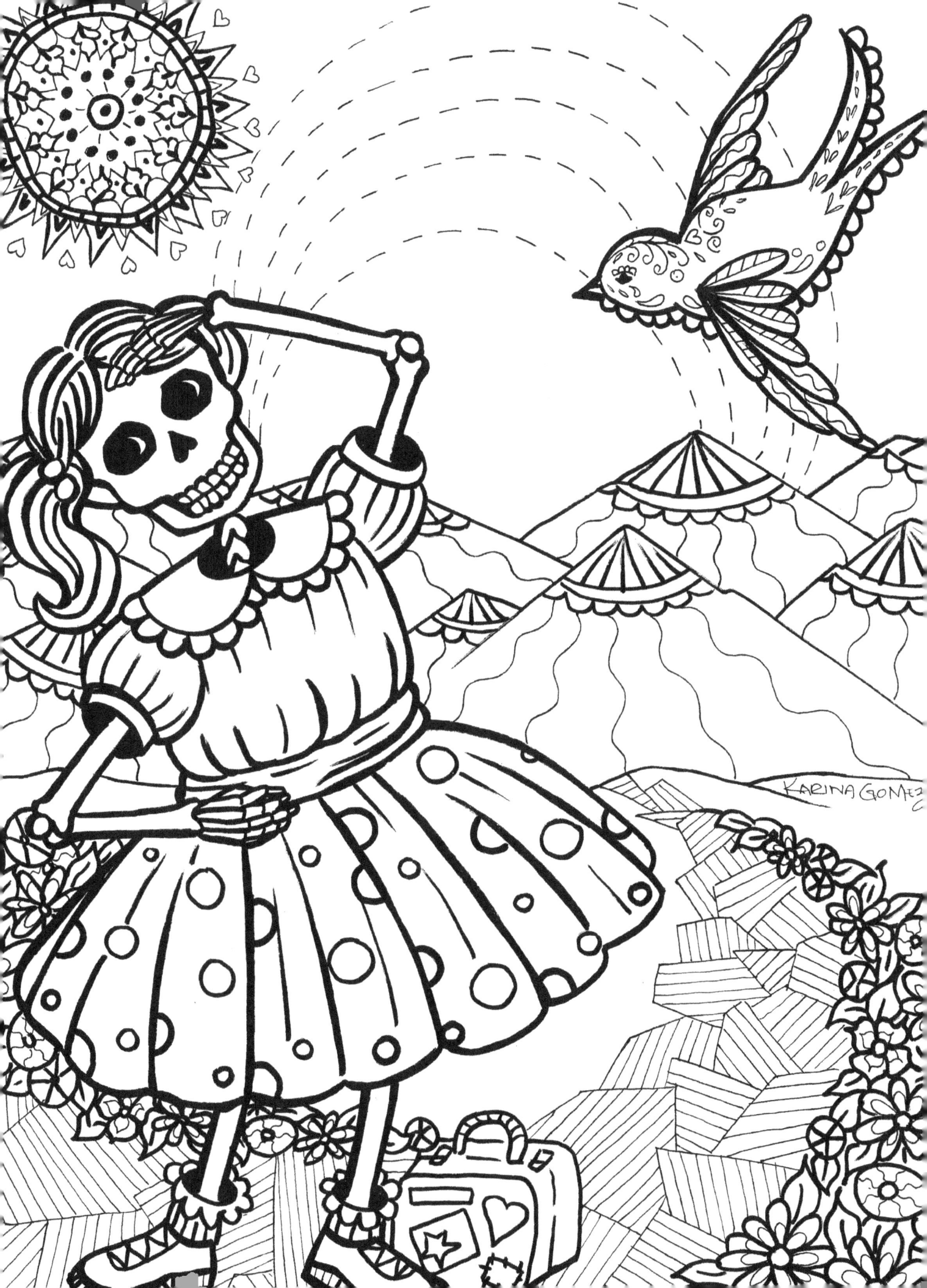

What makes you sing little bird?
Is it the lovely morning you so enjoy?
Tell me your secret lovely little bird,
Show me the song you so sweetly hum.

With so much pleading, he finally conceded
He bowed down and let me
hop on his feathered back
We flew high into the sky
So high that the clouds covered the ground
Up above the blue sky shared its silvery star

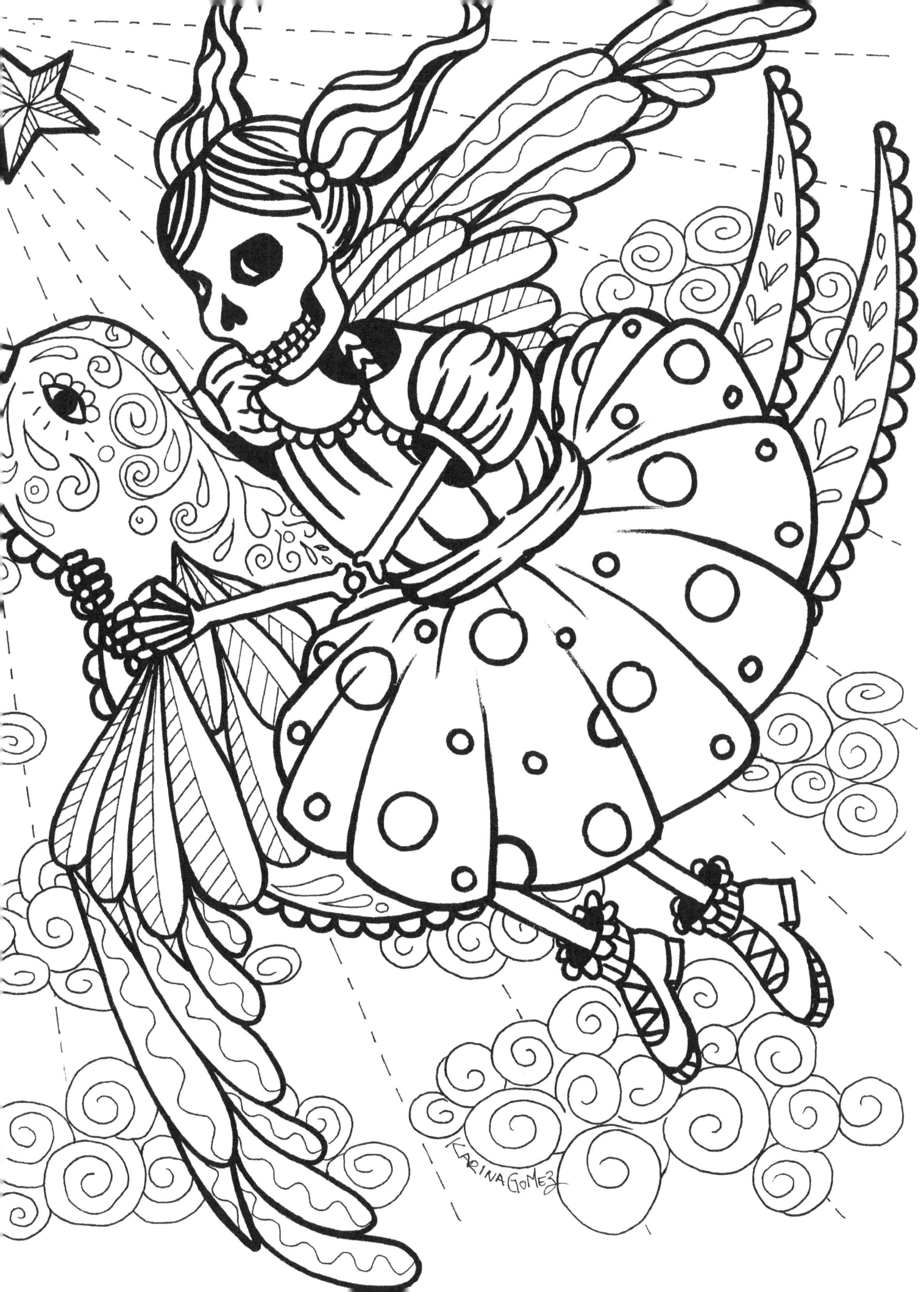

It shimmered and shined
The clouds were a sea of fluffy white
A sea of cotton sheep, side by side
They treaded the pillowy clouds
And ran to the other side of the majestic sky.

I turned to my lovely bird and asked,
"What is your secret, little bird?"
And then like the sound of church bells,
he sang this song:

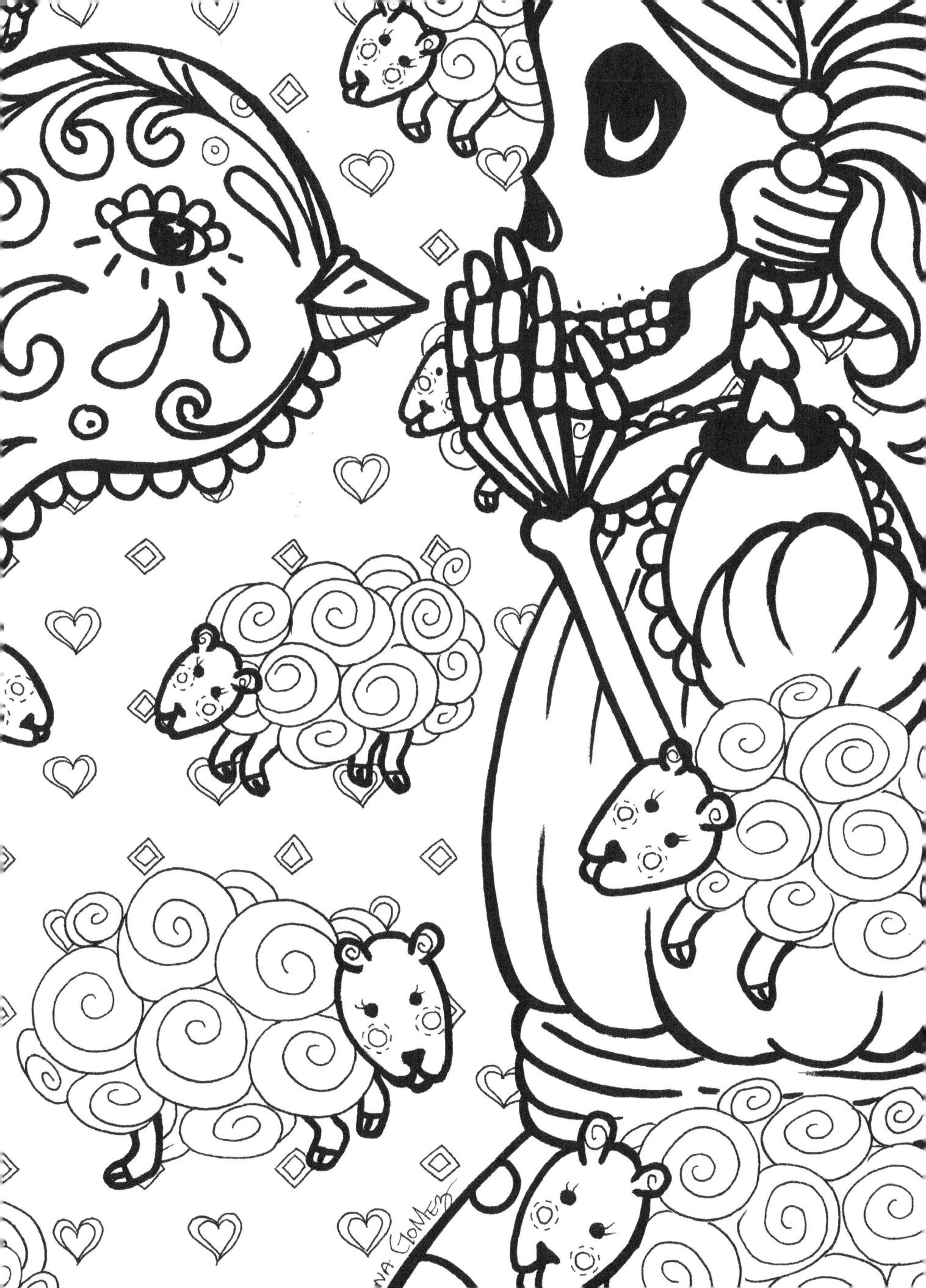

"A sweet melody of freedom lives in my heart;
I hope to share my sweet love song with you
Think of me always even when we're apart
And always when you see the sun."

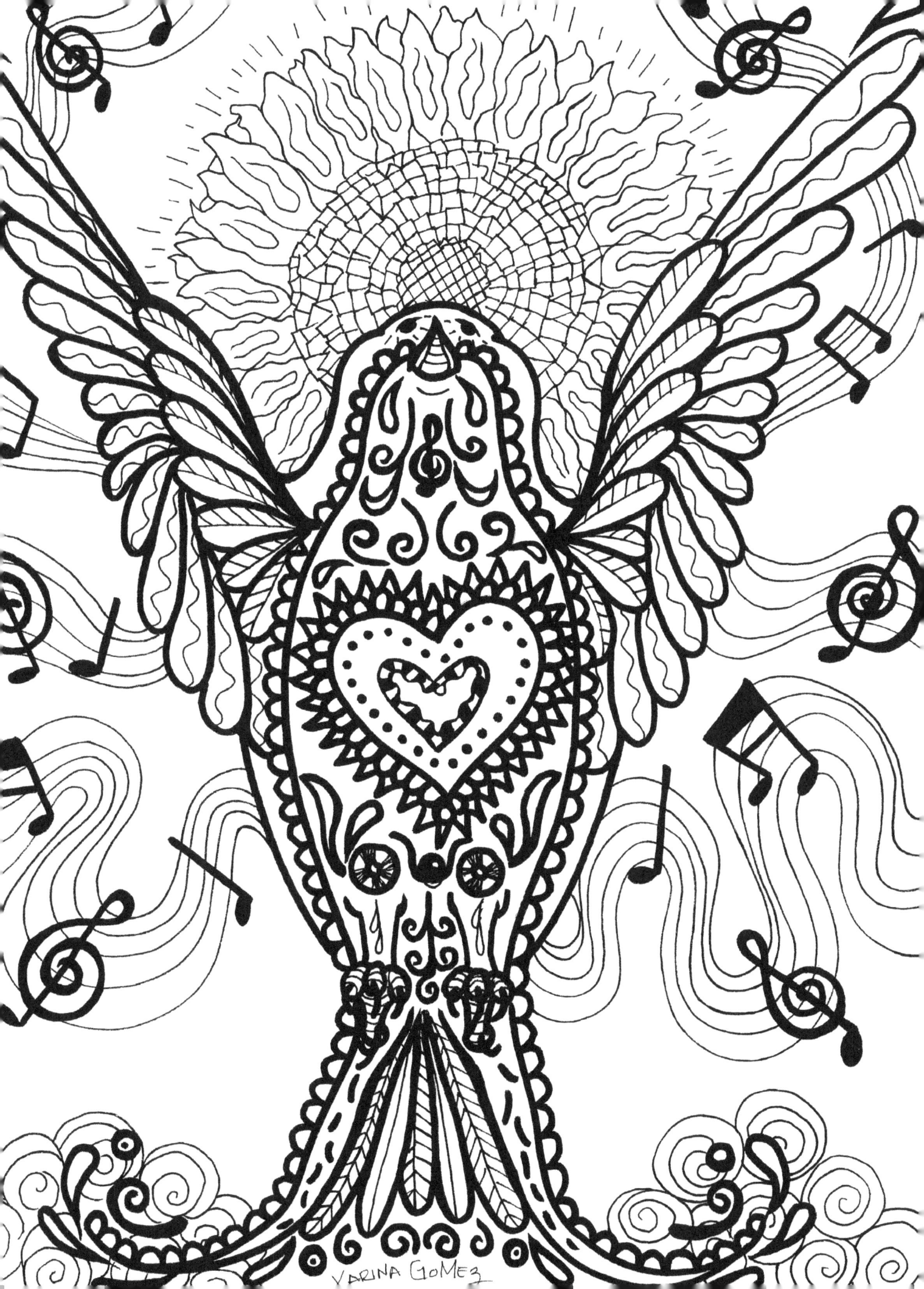

VARINA GOMEZ

Then he descended from the vast blue sky
Took me home
And with his little love song simply said,
Goodbye.

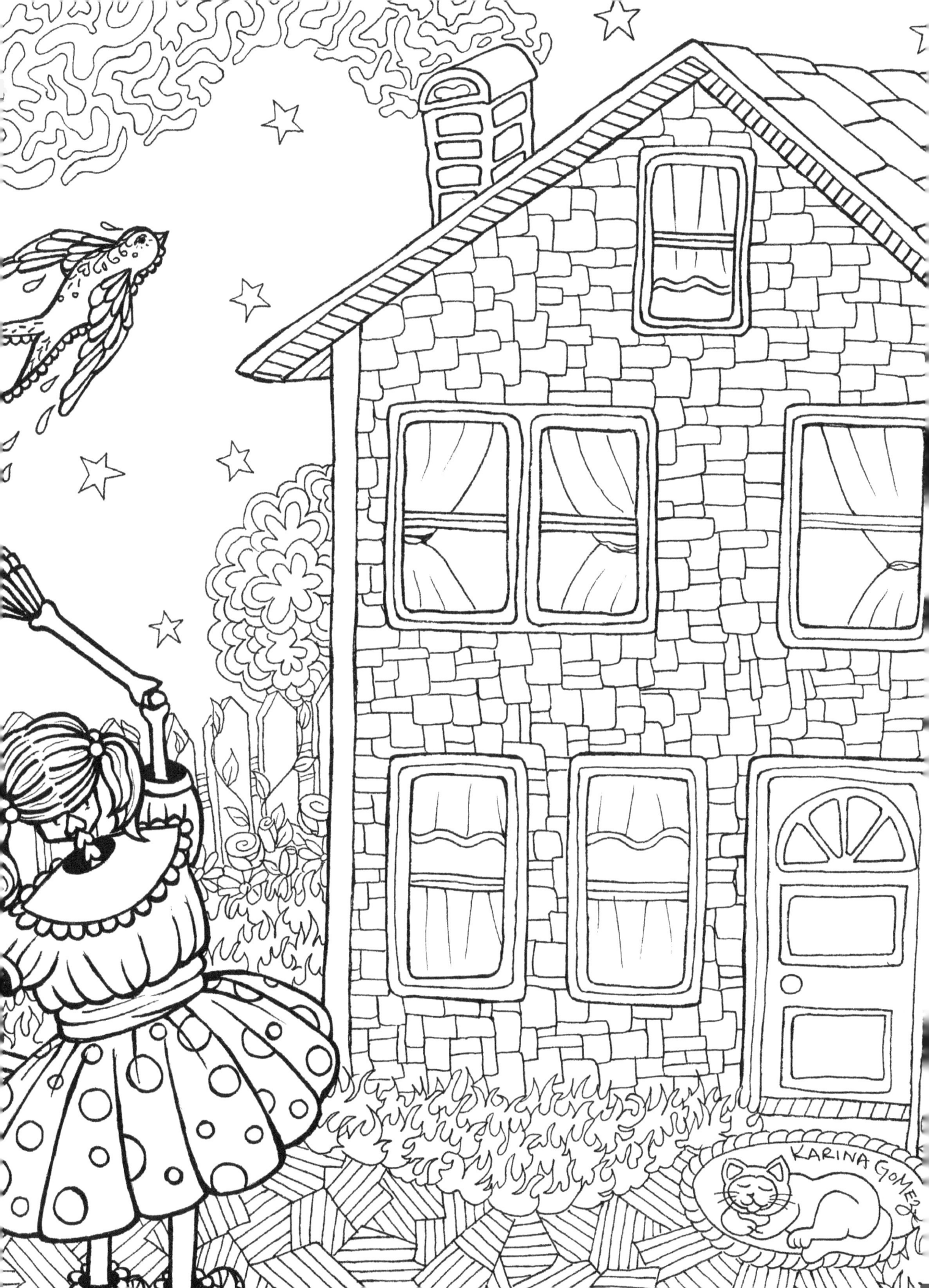

VIII

True Love

Just like a star that is born at
night And then withers away
In the morning light

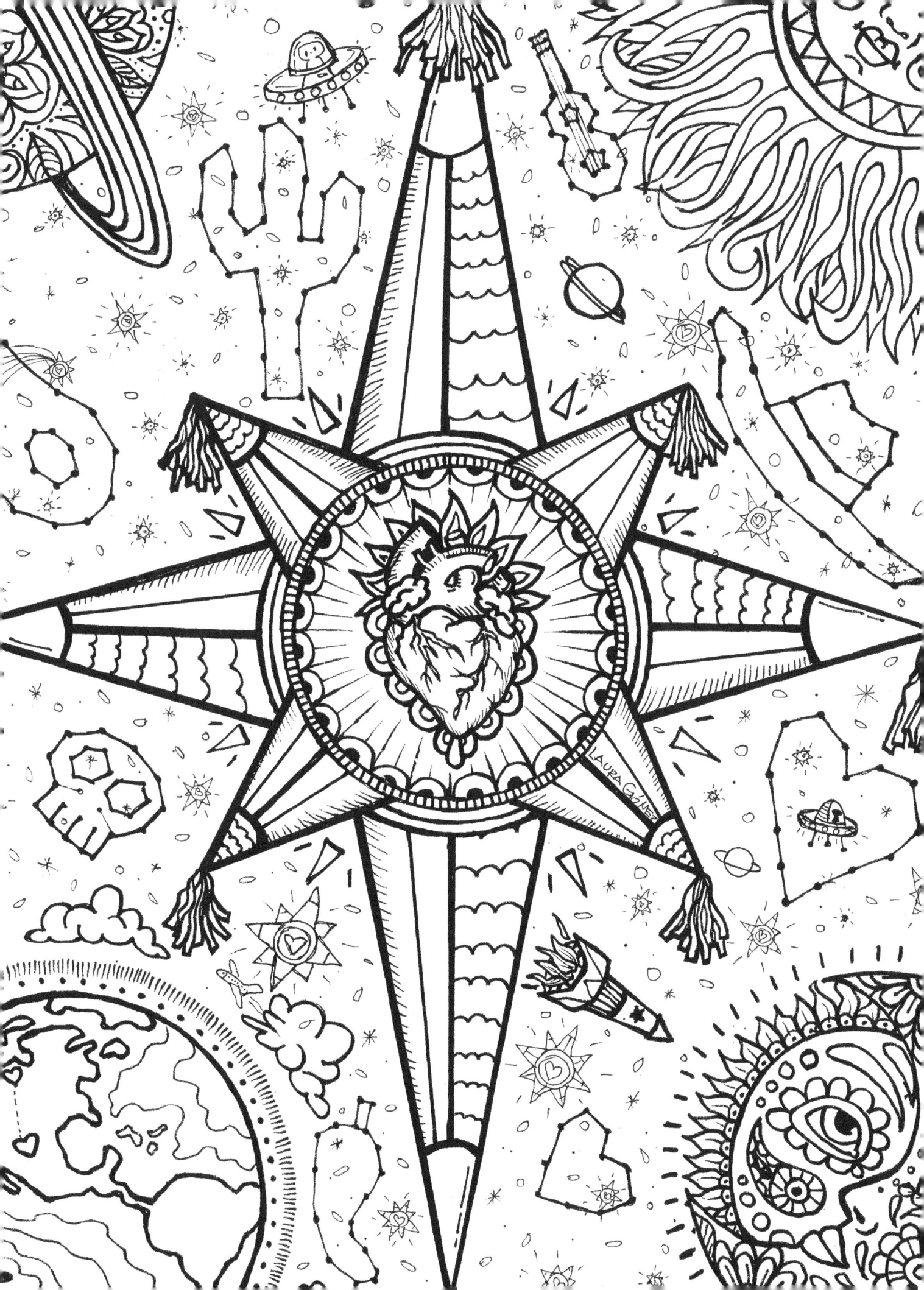

Are those arms that caressed you
And the kisses that rained on you

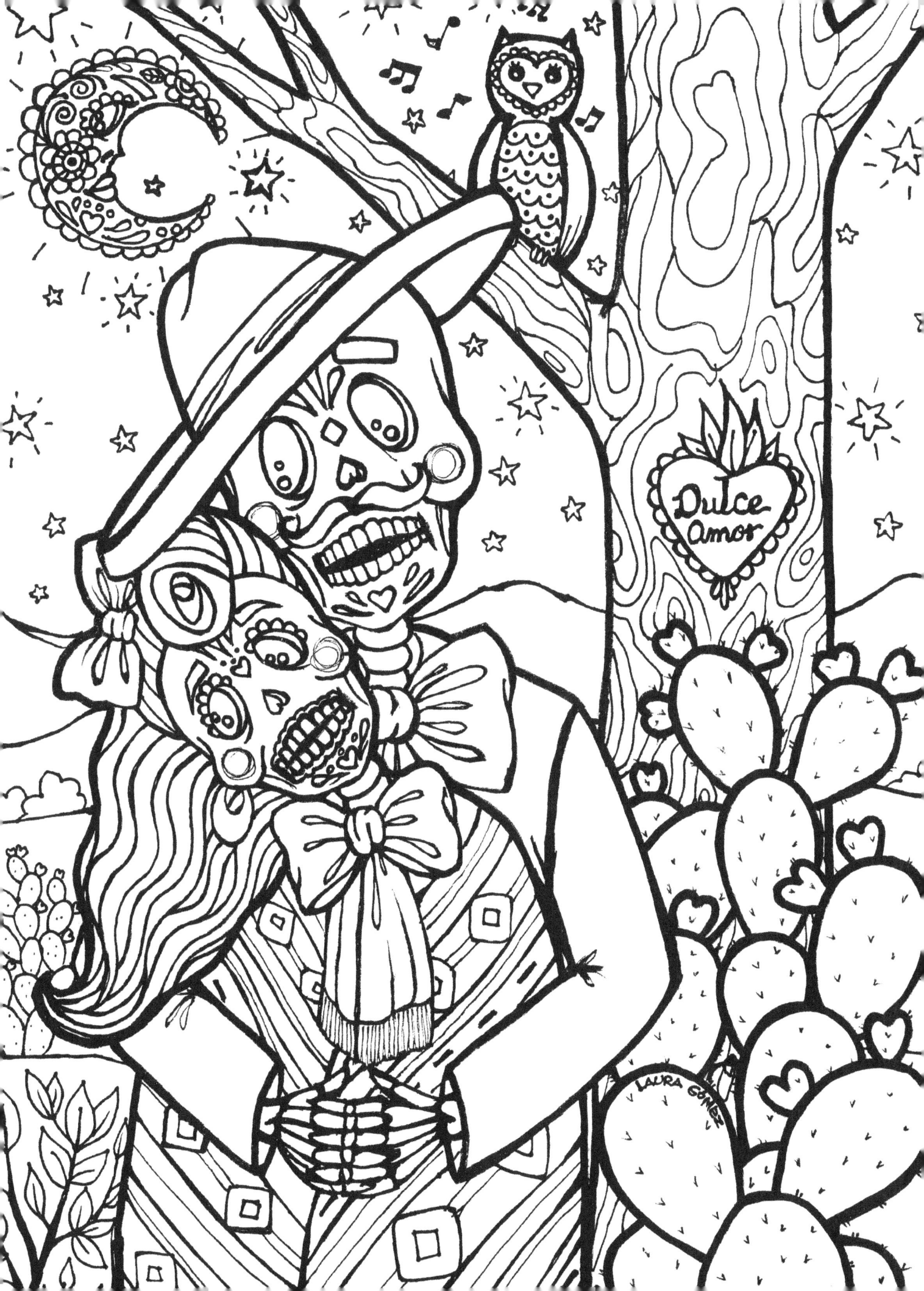

In a deceitful world
Where callousness can prevail
We find something pure
Something true, cordial and fair

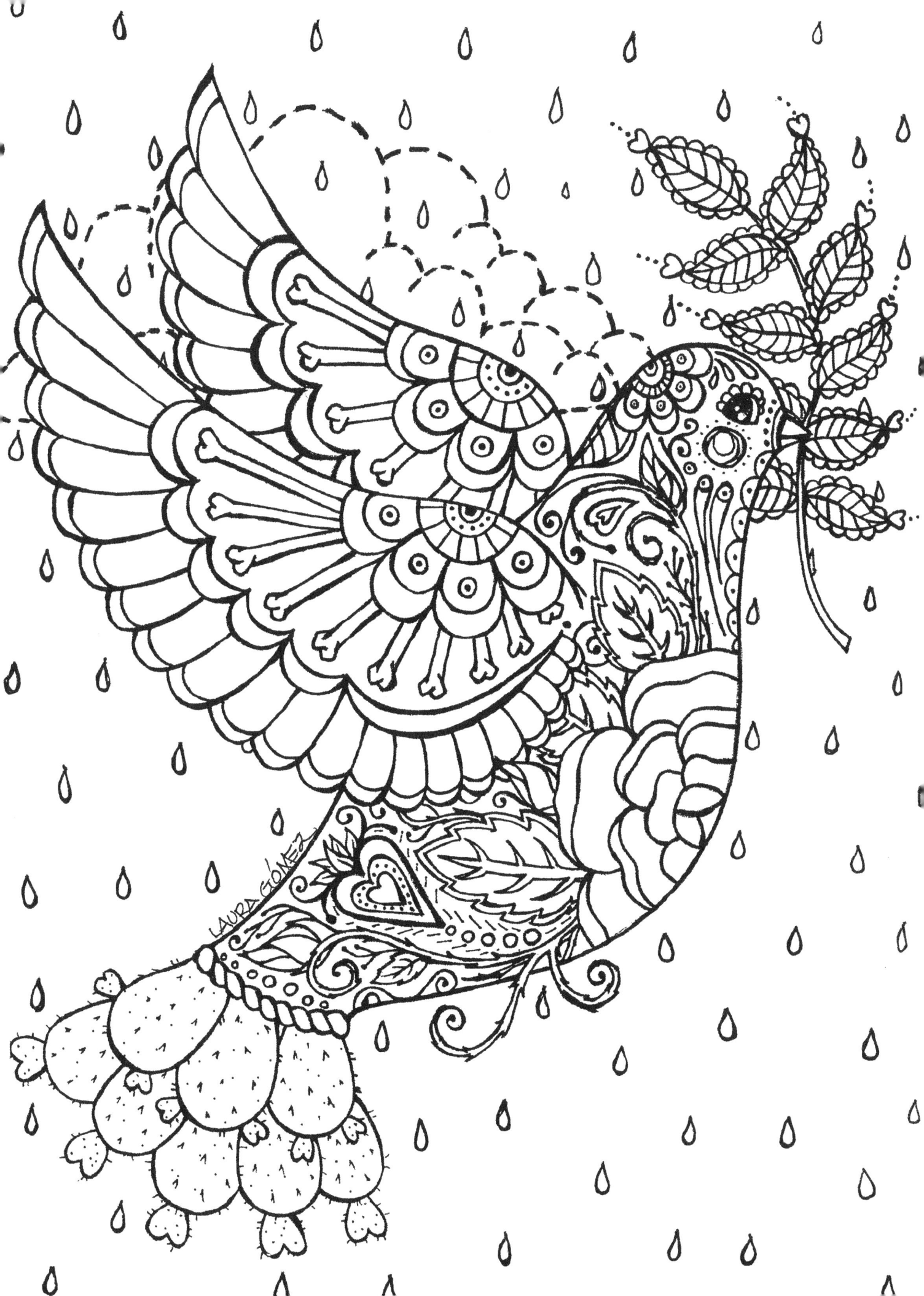

You can break the ice
That has frozen your hope
Of finding a love so pure
That others have let go
It's like the blood in your veins
Pumping into your heart

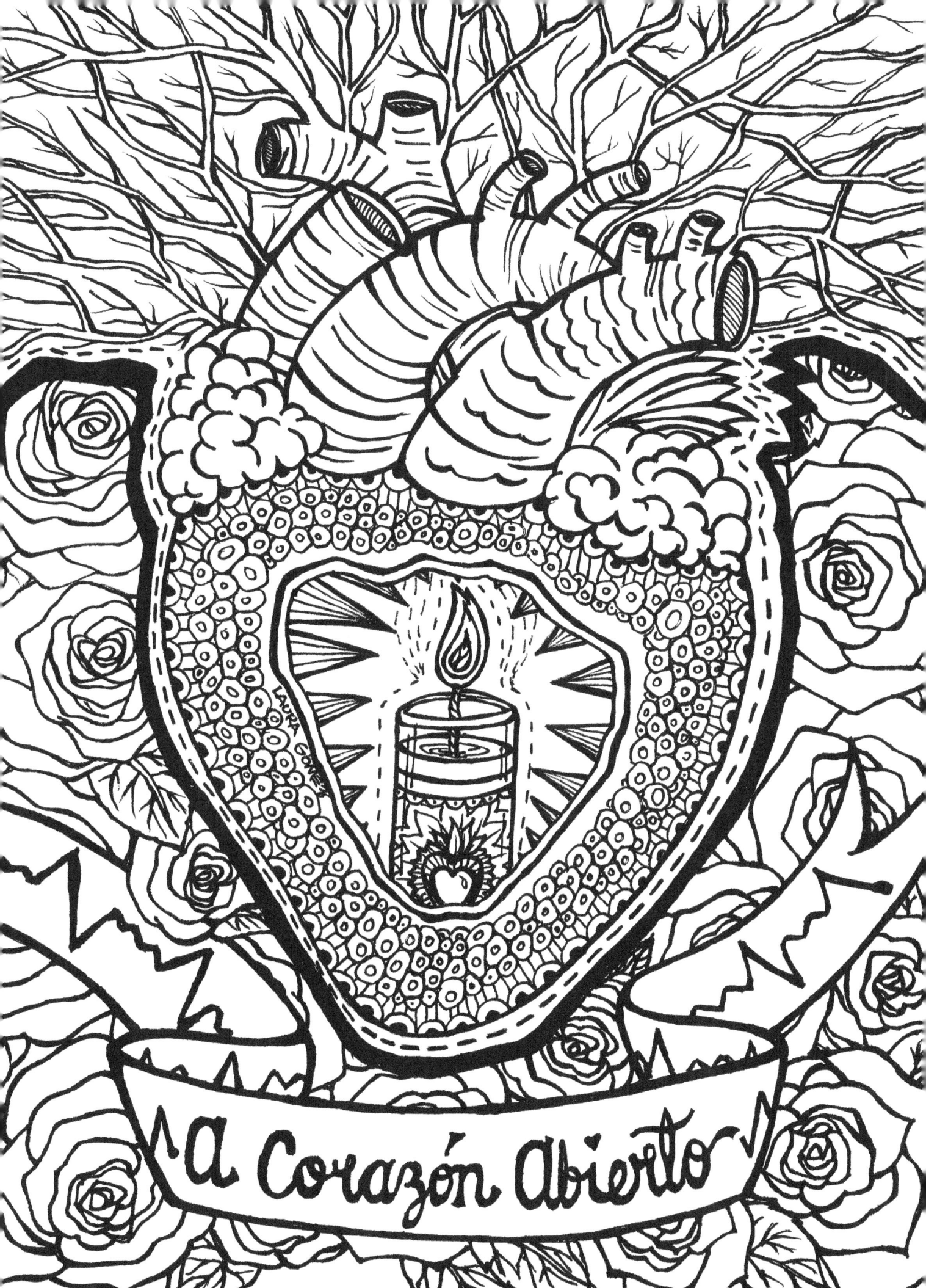

A Corazón Abierto

So much to give
So much to receive
If only you allow yourself
To finally give in

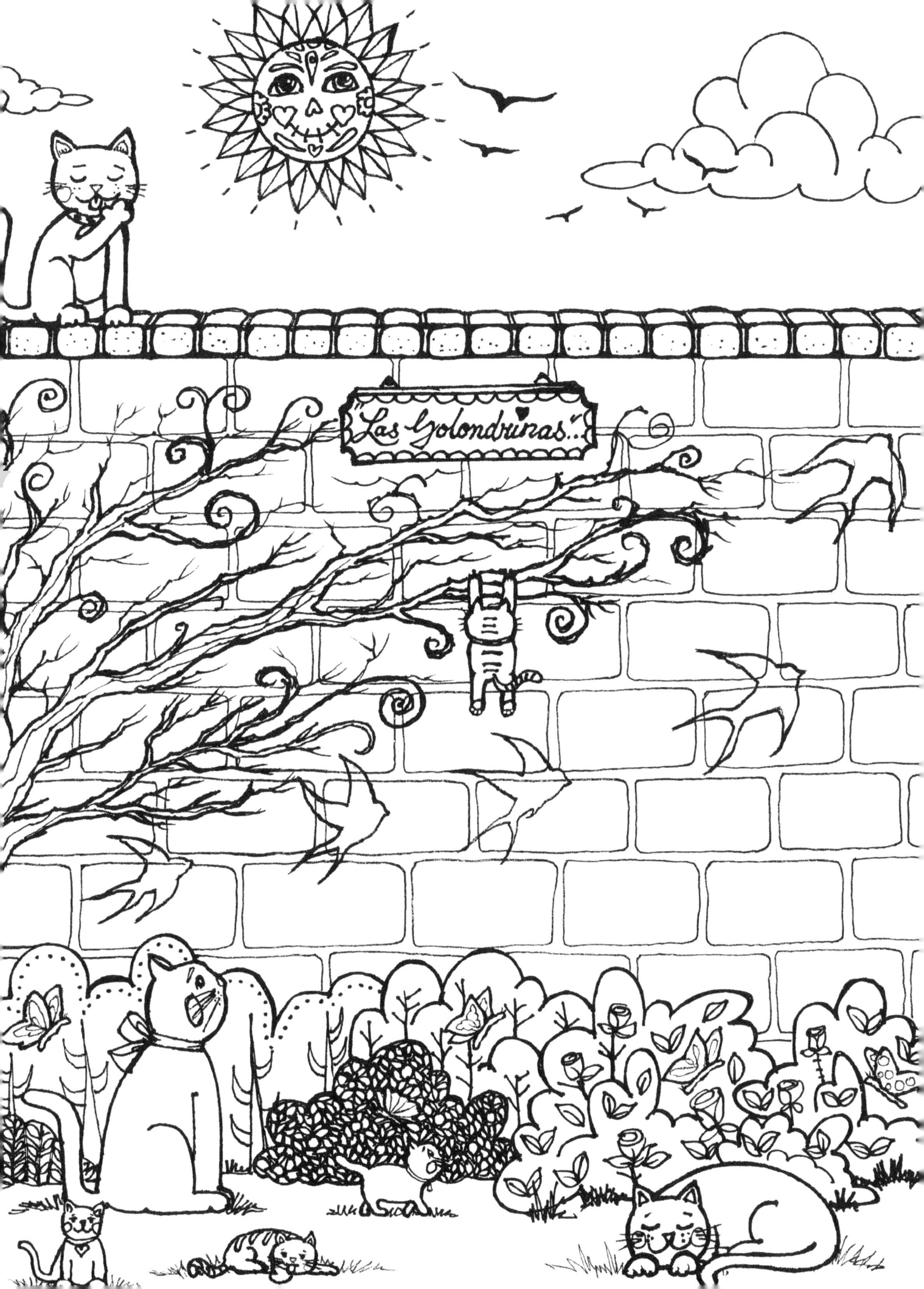

IX

The Family Quilt

The family quilt is made of a tapestry of color
Everyone has given a tiny piece of their soul
Even the garden, has given up some of its own

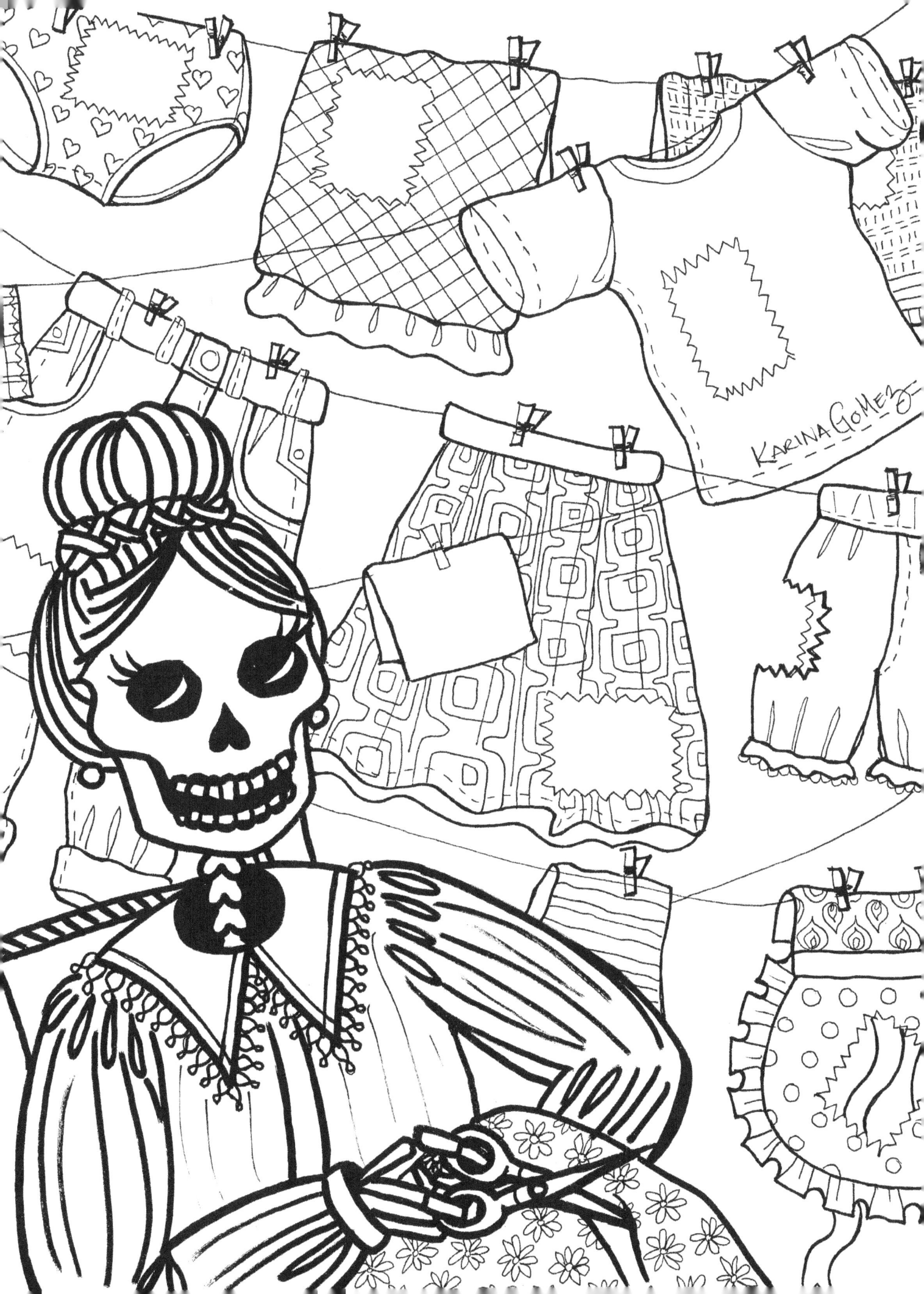

With diligent hands
While reminiscing about raising the kids
They would sew the pieces together
Until late at night when sleep would take over

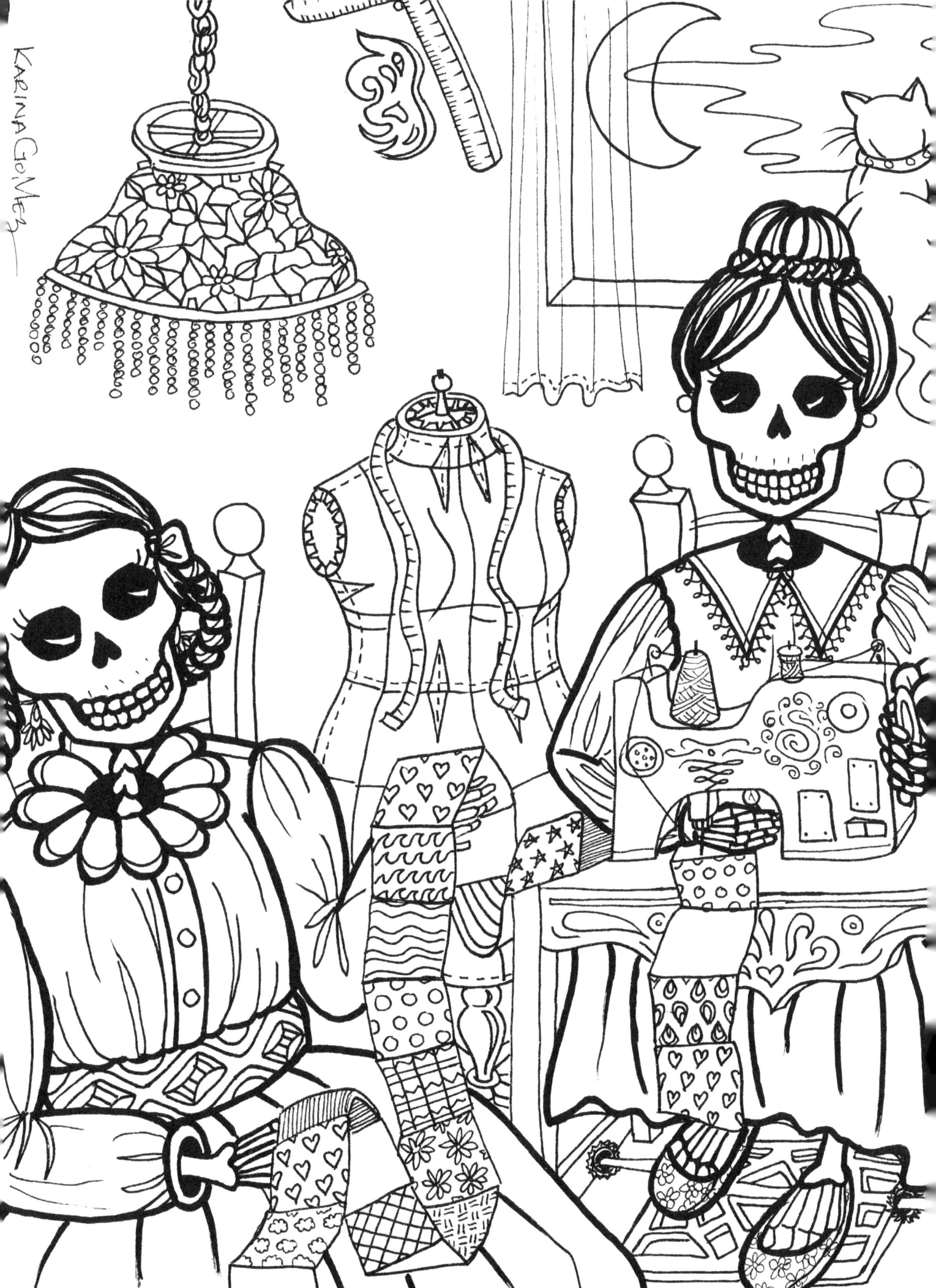

Over coffee they continued the tales
About children and spouses
Teardrops fell, laughs were had
All over those times past

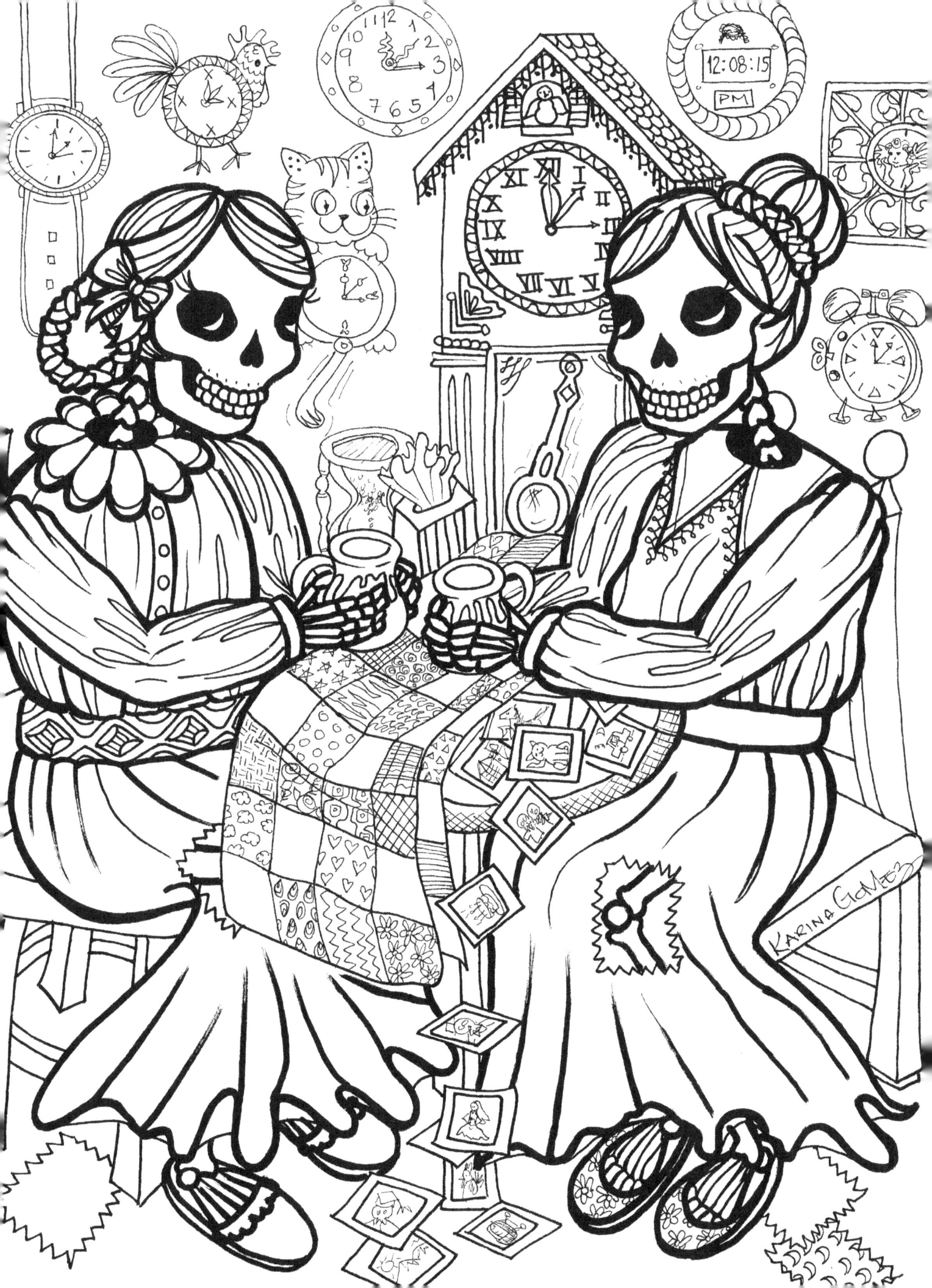

They continued the work of gathering the story
As they quilted the squares into the family treasure

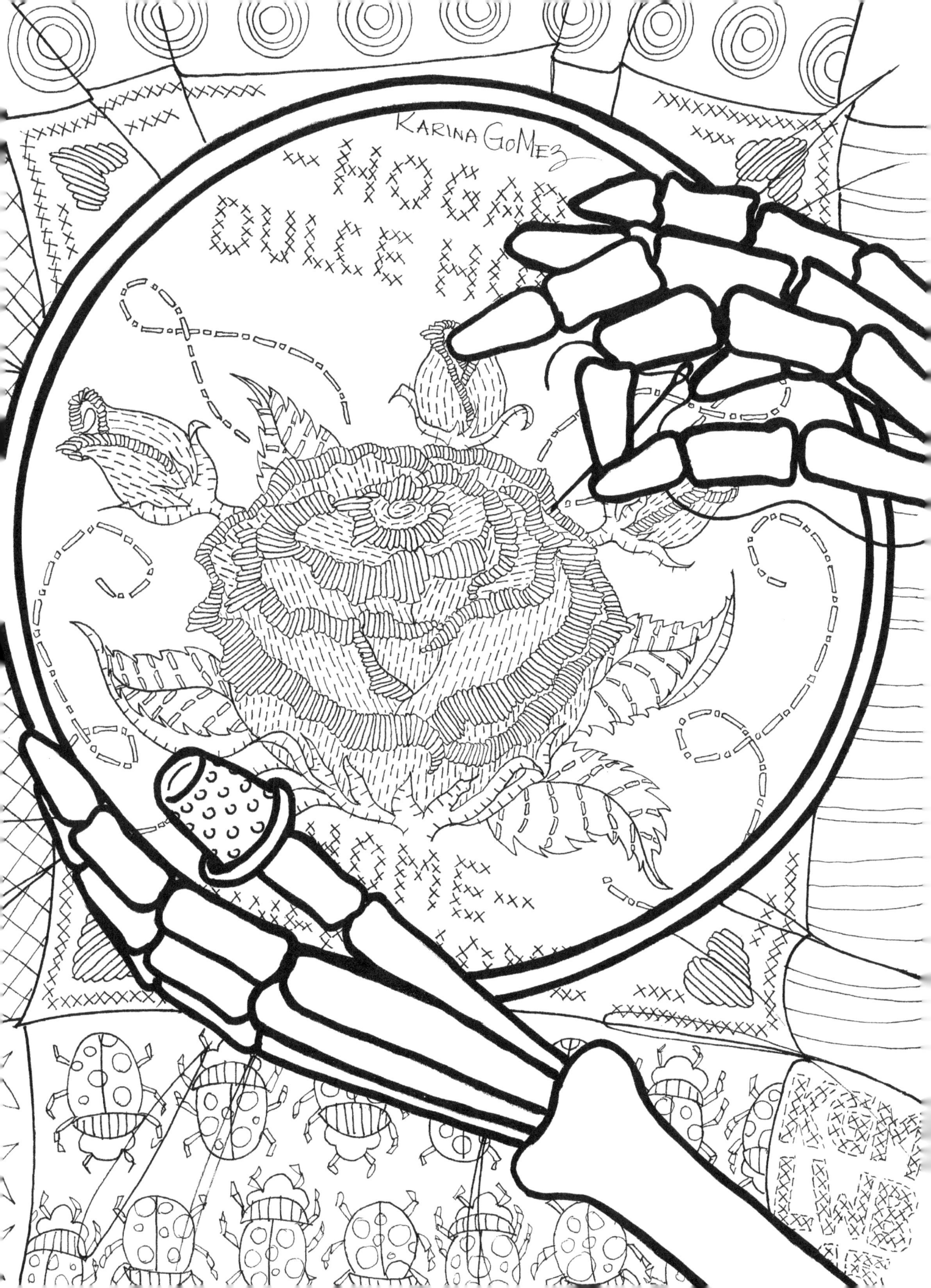

Each threaded square
Of the quilt tells our story
Our family history in all its glory.

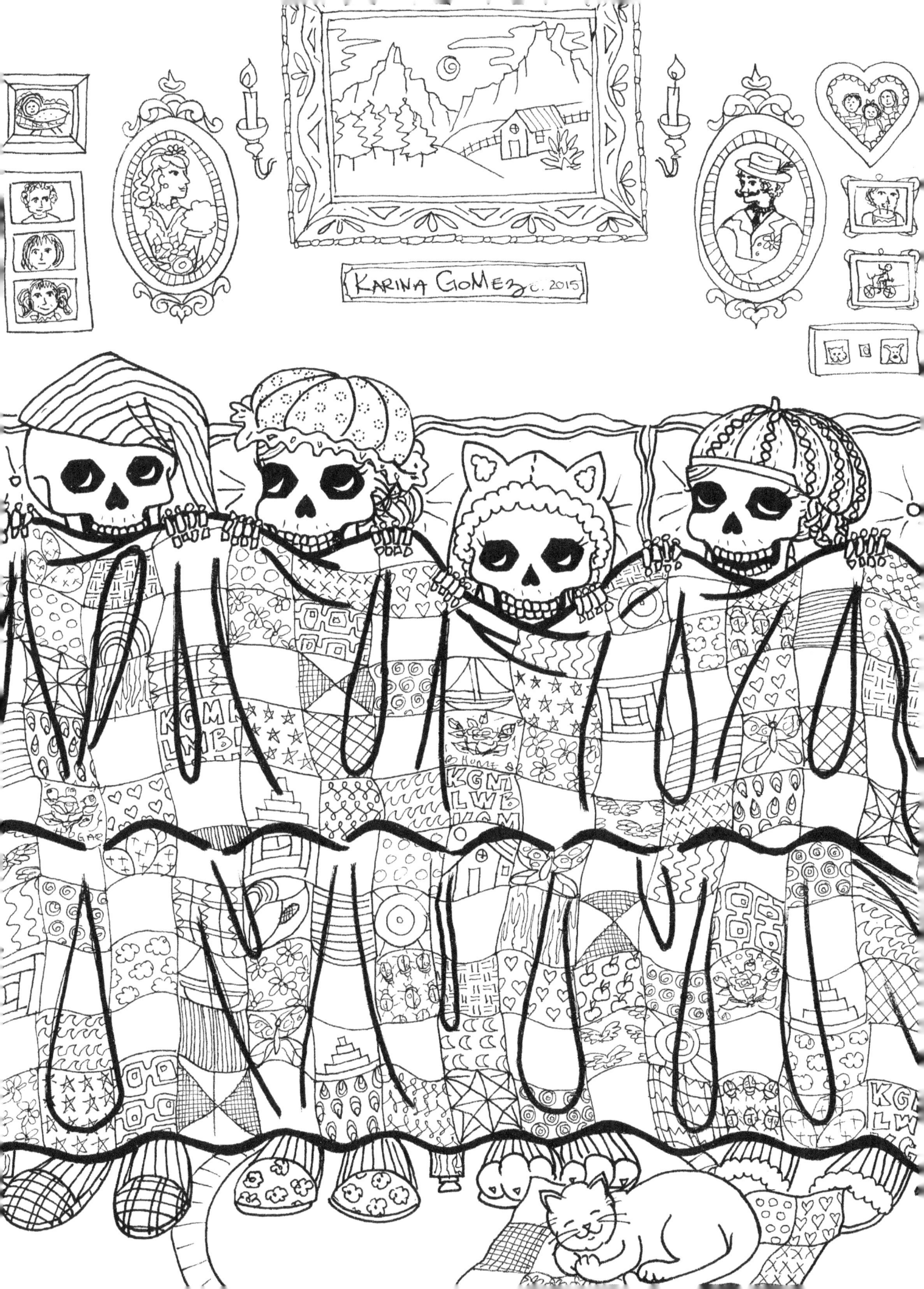

KARINA GÓMEZ

Karina's work is inspired by her family, life experiences and her Mexican culture. Her love of art was instilled in her by her father since she was a little girl. The Day of the Dead tradition was engrained in her memory while living across the street from a cemetery when she was 15 years old.

LAURA GÓMEZ

Laura was born in the city of Delicias in the state of Chihuahua in Mexico, where she also studied Communications and Business Administration. Currently, she resides in Chicago where she spends her time creating art, including abstract pieces, along with Mexican jewelry. She reaches for her paintbrush when words are not enough to express her emotions.

AMELIA OROZCO

Amelia was raised on both sides of the U.S./Mexican border. As such, both cultures are interwoven into her experience. Poetry has always been one way she has shared her stories, and has been able to relive those moments deeply rooted in her heart.

To see more art by Laura Gómez y Karina Gómez, visit colorfulculture.etsy.com.